Conspiracy
Ulster plots and plotters in 1615

THE ULSTER SOCIETY FOR IRISH HISTORICAL STUDIES.

The Ulster Society for Irish Historical Studies was founded in 1936 in order to promote the study of Irish history. For further information about the society's activities contact the secretary, c/o Dept. of Modern History, Queen's University, Belfast.

Other titles in this series, *Explorations in Irish history* include: *Edwardian Belfast: a social profile* by Sybil Gribbon; *Sin, Sheep and Scotsmen: John George Adair and the Derryveagh evictions* by W.E. Vaughan; *Living like a lord: the second marquis of Donegall, 1769-1844* by W.A. Maguire; *Ways to wealth: the Cust family of eighteenth century Armagh* by L.A. Clarkson and E.M. Crawford. The first three titles in the series were co-published with Appletree Press.

CONSPIRACY
Ulster plots and plotters in 1615

RAYMOND GILLESPIE

Ulster Society for Irish Historical Studies

Institute of Irish Studies, Queen's University, Belfast

ISBN 0 85389 303 9
First published 1987

The Ulster Society for Irish Historical Studies
c/o Dept. of Modern History, Queen's University, Belfast

Typesetting by Textflow Services Ltd.
Printed by W. & G. Baird Ltd.

Acknowledgements

I wish to acknowledge the generous financial assistance given by the Twenty Seven Foundation and the Department of Education, Northern Ireland towards the costs of publishing this essay. I also wish to acknowledge the Board of Trinity College, Dublin for permission to reproduce Cuconnacht O'Keenan's deposition, the Comptroller of Her Majesty's Stationery Office for permission to reproduce the 1622 maps of the Londonderry plantation by Thomas Raven and the Trustees of the National Library, Ireland for 1602 map of Charlemount. I am grateful to a large number of people for advice and assistance while writing this essay but especially to Mary Cunningham, Peter Folan, and John McLoughlin for their help in translating texts and to Bernadette Cunningham for her help in interpreting the Irish language sources. Brian Jackson was kind enough to draw my attention to the Jesuit Annual Letter of 1615 which mentioned the conspiracy and David Sheehy searched diligently in the Dublin Diocesan Archive for the papers relating to the early twentieth century cause of the Irish martyrs. It would be impossible to record here the less tangible contributions of many people who made suggestions or listened to versions of the story told here but, as with all works on the history of Ulster, the invisible hand of Dr W. H. Crawford has left a deep impression. Even with this help the essay would not have appeared without the support of the Ulster Society for Irish Historical Studies, particularly Dr Margaret Crawford, and the Institute of Irish Studies, Queen's University, Belfast, especially Dr Brian Walker.

Contents

Acknowledgements   v

List of illustrations   vi

Prologue: the bishop makes his will   1

1. A conspiracy is announced   3

2. The plots   13

3. The plotters   25

4. The trial   43

5. From traitors to saints   51

List of Illustrations

Sir Arthur Chichester   4

The deposition of Cuconnacht O'Keenan
(Trinity College Library)   8

The estate of the Merchant Tailors, c. 1622   14

The town of Coleraine, c. 1622   17

The town of Derry, c. 1622   21

Charlemount fort, c. 1602   23

Sir Thomas Phillips's castle of Limavady, c. 1622   31

Sir Hugh O'Neill, earl of Tyrone   39

Tim Healy   58

Prologue: The Bishop Makes His Will

Of all the powerful intellects and witty writers who surrounded Jonathan Swift, the dean of Saint Patrick's Cathedral, in the Dublin of the early eighteenth century, none was to leave such an imposing mark on the capital city as John Stearne, bishop of Clogher. When he made his will on 13 May 1741 he left money to build the steeple on top of the tower of Saint Patrick's, which is still a prominent local landmark. His building activities were not confined to the cathedral since in 1721 he had given money to Trinity College, Dublin, of which he was vice chancellor, to build the printing house which also still stands. The College also benefited in other ways. He bequeathed to the college any books which he owned that were not already in the College library, the remainder going to Archbishop Marsh's library, at Saint Patrick's Cathedral.

To Trinity College library he also left his large manuscript collection. Most of his collection had been bought from Dr John Madden who had, in turn, acquired the bulk of it from Matthew Barry, the clerk of the Irish Privy Council in the 1670s and 1680s. This was an age when official papers were not yet regarded as the property of the state but rather of the official who had used them and Barry, who had assembled them, had been at the centre of many of the most important developments of the late seventeenth century. Thus the collection of manuscripts bequeathed to Trinity College was important for the light which the documents shed on the history of seventeenth century Ireland and includes, for instance, the depositions taken in the aftermath of the rebellion of 1641.

Not only was the collection important, it was also large, so large indeed that the College had to build a new cupboard, press F, in which to store it. On the third shelf of this new cupboard John Lyon, a canon of St Patrick's and one of the foremost antiquarians of his day, who was arranging the collection, placed as the fifteenth item a small book which he called 'Plantation Papers'. It was in fact a miscellaneous collection of twenty items bound together and ranging in date from the mid-sixteenth century to the 1680s.

One item within the volume was a small book, poorly preserved, of thirty-two pages. When the volume was rebound in vellum by John Exshaw of Dublin in 1743, at a cost of 2*s.* 4*d.*, the first three pages and four pages in the middle were already missing. This small book is a near contemporary transcript of depositions and examinations taken after the discovery in April 1615 of a plot for a native Irish rising in Ulster. Most of the originals are now lost, but two have survived among the State papers in the Public Record Office, London having been sent to the Privy Council by the lord deputy, Arthur Chichester, in April 1615 together with a letter announcing the discovery of the plot.[1]

The survival of the transcripts, which we owe to the antiquarian concern of Bishop Stearne, provides a window through which we can glimpse something of the hopes and fears of those who lived in Ulster in the early years of the plantation scheme in the province. These depositions give a perspective which would not be revealed to us in the official records of the central administration or in the formal records of the great estates. Inevitably, many of our glimpses are oblique and not as clearly focused as we would wish. But rather than be disappointed by the incomplete nature of the evidence, we should relish the rare opportunity of reading over the shoulder of the takers of the depositions and looking for the facts which they never intended to tell us but, almost inadvertently, revealed.

1. A Conspiracy is Announced

At eight o'clock on the morning of Tuesday 18 April 1615 the third session of James I's first Irish parliament reassembled in Dublin Castle after an adjournment of almost five months. In the House of Lords it was a slow start. The only business to be done was the recording of the death of the old tenth earl of Ormonde, 'Black Tom', and the issuing of a writ of summons requiring his nephew, Walter, the eleventh earl, to take his uncle's seat. In the Commons the attorney general and speaker, Sir John Davies, opened the session with prayers of thanks and writs were issued for the seats which had become vacant because of the death of three members during the recess. Little other business could be done because the only bill to have arrived from England was that for the imposition of taxation, the subsidy, and it was likely to prove controversial. Moreover, the clerk of the Commons, William Bradley, was ill. The House adjourned for two days but not before it had instructed the Privy Councillors who were also M.P.s to request an audience with the King's representative in Ireland, the lord deputy, Sir Arthur Chichester. A long memorandum on the state of Ireland had been submitted to him at the end of the second session in November 1614 and the Commons were anxious for the deputy's reply.[2]

Later that day an audience was granted and Chichester gave his replies to the points raised by the Commons and thanked them for the way in which business had been conducted in the last session. The thanks was in many ways hollow since the orderly conduct of business had been part of the plan of the recusant opposition to place the king under an obligation to them. The tactics of disruption which they had employed during the first session in an attempt to gain administrative reforms to ameliorate the position of the Catholic Old English of the Pale had backfired on them and created only aggravation. James summoned them to London to express his displeasure by deeming them 'half subjects'. This was not the desired result since the Old English maintained that despite their catholicism they were loyal to the pope only in spiritual matters and that their allegiance in temporal matters lay with the crown. A good relationship with the crown was vital since the king was the final court of appeal for them. As power

The Right Honble Right Wise and Valiant ARTHUR LO CHICHESTER,
L.O. Baron of Belfast, Lo. High Treasurer of Ireland, *and sometimes*
Lo: Deputy *of that* Kingdom *à* 11 *years & upward.*
One of the Privy Counsell in ENGLAND.

The above Inscription is round the Oval of the Original.

Sir Arthur Chichester, lord deputy of Ireland 1604-15.

became increasingly concentrated in the New English settler administration in Ireland the Old English and the native Irish communities, who found themselves excluded, gradually came to see the king in London as a valuable counterweight to the growing power of the New English.

At this point in the audience Chichester revealed what he thought would be his trump card in the management of the early weeks of the new session of parliament. He had discovered a plot in Ulster, had seized the chief conspirators and had informed the English Privy Council of his discovery the same day. The plot involved a 'pack of dangerous conspirators' who had planned to seize the newly-built forts and garrison towns of Ulster, Coleraine, Londonderry and Carrickfergus; to release Con O'Neill, the son of the earl of Tyrone, from Charlemount where he was kept and, more ambitious still, to overthrow the recently established Ulster plantation.[3]

The reactions to this news, as they emerged over the last week of April 1615, were varied. Sir Robert Jacob, the Irish solicitor general, writing to Sir Ralph Winwood, the principal secretary of state in England, on 28 April was inclined to dismiss the whole affair.[4] It was, he thought, a matter of no importance and he considered that some men were blowing the matter up out of all proportion. He was not the only one to express such a view. Winwood's own secretary, Francis Blundell, who was a member of the Irish parliament and a landowner in Wexford, had written a similar letter to his master two days earlier, although the letter had been delayed since the ships to England could not sail because of adverse winds.[5] Blundell was more forthright in his accusations than Jacob. He had made enquiries about the plot but could find out nothing. He was convinced that Chichester was deliberately suppressing information about the plot to encourage rumour and speculation so that the conspiracy would appear to be more dangerous than it actually was.

There was probably a large measure of truth in Blundell's and Jacob's assessment of the situation when they argued that the conspiracy was being over-rated. Lord Deputy Chichester's plan, by his own admission, was to use the plot as an excuse to prorogue the parliament as a matter of urgency. He argued that this would allow the members who were also army officers and government officials in Ulster to return to the province to carry out a follow-up operation to track down any further traitors or plots. However, before parliament could be prorogued in this way the subsidy bill would have to be passed because the dates for issuing the writs for the collection of the subsidy, which were set out in the bill, would have passed if it were not enacted almost immediately. The passage of the subsidy bill was the main piece of business which the king had appointed for the third session of the parliament. As early as March 1615 Chichester had been instructed by the king that if the subsidy bill would pass in the third session then the session could be continued but if it was not likely to receive the assent the parliament was to be dissolved.[6] It was thought the passage of the subsidy bill would be contentious, and that the opposition would use the occasion to extract concessions from the government in return for support for the bill. If Chichester could only engineer a national crisis as an excuse for proroguing the troublesome parliament it might be possible to force the bill through quickly before the prorogation.

The grant of some taxation was essential since the Irish government was effectively bankrupt. There had been no grant of taxation since the 1580s and government expenditure was vastly greater than its income. In 1612, for example, government income stood at about £24,000 and expenditure was £33,000. This broke down into roughly £13,000 for civil expenditure and the balance for the army, which was deemed necessary for the protection of the kingdom.[7] The shortfall between revenue and expenditure was provided by treasure sent from England which was invariably too little, too late. Most of what had been sent in 1615, for instance, had been used up in paying off past debts and the expenses of the parliament leaving little for current expenditure. As a result the army was infrequently paid and more frequently discontented. As Chichester himself put it, Ireland was living from hand to mouth. Clearly this situation could not continue indefinitely.[8]

Ireland's deficit was underwritten by supplies of money from England yet, there, royal finances were far from healthy, especially after the debacle of the 'Addled parliament' which had lasted for just six weeks in April and May 1614 and had broken up in disorder without voting a subsidy. Ireland, rather than providing the storehouse of wealth as promised by the early seventeenth-century advocates of plantation, was costing the crown money it could ill afford. As an exasperated member of the English Addled parliament of 1614 complained 'Ireland is not a thorn in our foot but a lance in our side. If [there is] a revolt there what shame and disgrace would it be either to leave [it] or misery to recover it.'[9]

Since so much of the Irish expenditure was on the army, which was regarded as essential for defence against the native Irish who, it was feared, might rise at any moment, the only way to balance the books was to increase the revenue from within Ireland. However the passage of a subsidy bill was not an easy matter. The government feared that the Catholic recusant opposition, which had shown its ability to organise, to outwit, and to outvote the government in the second session of the parliament, would use the occasion to exact concessions for Catholics from the government. They would block the bill because they felt their best chance of securing concessions was to keep the parliament in session. Indeed this was the tactic of the recusants for as John Sutton, the Catholic member for Kildare, commented during the debate on the subsidy bill:

> Little said soon amended,
> subsidy granted, the parliament ended'.[10]

Chichester's use of the discovery of the conspiracy may not have produced the desired effect – a quick passage of the subsidy bill and a dissolution of parliament – but it did ensure that the subsidy bill was passed with remarkable speed despite the opposition of the recusants. It was introduced into the Commons on 22 April and passed by 28 April: only five sitting days. It was a speed which surprised even the king who made a number of concessions to the recusant members as a reward for the speed of passage of the bill.[11] The atmosphere which Chichester had created ensured that the former apathy of the New English members, which had given the opposition their chance to control the business of the second session of the parliament, had been effectively dissipated and a new urgency had been brought to parliamentary business.

This reaction of the M.P.s is some evidence that the scepticism of Blundell and Jacob about the reality of the threat of rebellion was not shared by all. The English Privy Council took the matter very seriously indeed. No doubt their concern was sharpened by the fact that the king, James I, had been shown Chichester's correspondence. The experience of the Gunpowder Plot of 1604 and the Franceschi Plot of 1605, fresh in the minds of contemporaries, had left the king with a pathological fear of plots and plotters of all kinds. On 3 May 1615 the Council replied to Chichester's letter informing them of the discovery of the plot and they congratulated him for his care and vigilance.[12] The Irish Society, which was the body responsible for the Londonderry plantation where the plot was uncovered, was not so well treated. It was reprimanded for not strengthening the defences of Coleraine and Derry. In reply, the Society pleaded poverty.

As an additional measure the Privy Council asked Chichester to speed up the implementation of earlier plans to bring the sons of native Irish gentry to London for their education. In this way, it was argued, the upcoming generation could be made into proper English gentlemen and would forsake their barbarous ways, including, of course, conspiring against the Dublin administration.

Despite his opportunistic use of the conspiracy for political ends Chichester himself took it seriously. One measure of how seriously he took the conspiracy was that he was prepared to use judicial torture to extract information from one of the alleged conspirators, Cuconnacht

'The voluntary confession of Cowonnaght O'Kennan upon the racke'. Above it is the deposition of Gory Mac Manus O'Cahan with George Sexton, Chichester's secretary, acting as interpreter and Dominic Sarsfield, later a judge at the plotters trial, as a witness.

O'Keenan. Unlike England, the use of judicial torture was rare in early modern Ireland. No rack had existed in sixteenth-century Ireland, a subject of frequent administrative complaint, and when judicial torture was administered, as in the case of Bishop Dermot O'Hurley in 1583, other methods had to be found. Indeed O'Keenan may have the dubious distinction of being the first man racked in Ireland. It is not clear why he was accorded this singular honour since, as we shall see, he was only marginally involved in the plot. However, Cuconnacht was a brother of Tadhg O'Keenan, who with his relations had fled with the Earls of Tyrone and Tyrconnell in 1607, and so Cuconnacht was already under suspicion. Only two other cases of the use of a rack are known from the early seventeenth century: Owen O'Byrne and a Mr Mulvany both in 1627.

There was even confusion in the early seventeenth century as to the procedure to be followed for the administration of judicial torture. Torture lay outside the scope of the common law and hence permission for its administration had to be sought from the king or, more usually, the Privy Council. In Ireland, because of the country's peculiar constitutional status, the position was less clear. Was the granting of permission the role of the lord deputy, as the king's representative, the Irish Privy Council, the English Privy Council, or the king himself? In the case of O'Hurley in 1583 the permission had been given by the English Privy Council and in 1615 O'Keenan was racked by the authority of the lord deputy's commission, but by the 1620s the matter was less clear-cut.[13] It was complexities such as these which resulted in the very infrequent use of judicial torture in early modern Ireland. Thus the fact that it was used in 1615 points to the seriousness with which the activities of the Ulster plotters were viewed by the Dublin government.

The reason why the conspiracy was taken so seriously by the Dublin administrators lies in the fact that for some years they had been expecting just such a conspiracy. One roughly contemporary discourse on the settlement of the native Irish in Ulster under the plantation scheme assumed that if the native Irish were left there for any length of time plots and other mischief would naturally follow. From 3 September 1607 when Hugh O'Neill, earl of Tyrone, and his associates fled to continental Europe the government entertained the possibility that he would return to overthrow the plantation scheme which had been put in place in Ulster following the confiscation of the lands of the exiles. Within eight months of Tyrone's departure the rumours of his return were already circulating. As a result O'Neill's movements in Europe were carefully monitored by the English embassy at Brussels and other centres.

There were periodic scares of rebellion. In early 1613, for example,

Art og Mac Mahon, a son of Sir Bryan Mac Mahon a prominent
Monaghan landowner, was supposed to have revealed a plot for a
rebellion to the Fermanagh settler Sir John Wishart. Art was
summoned to Dublin but it transpired that the plot was no more than a
general grumbling 'that they [the native Irish] would be rid of the
British undertakers' and no armed rebellion seems to have been
planned.[14]

The reality of what could happen following Tyrone's return was
evident to most settlers in Ulster. In comparison with the native Irish
the settlers were in a minority, albeit a dominant one. In 1613, for
example, there was only between 2,000 and 2,240 adult British males
in the six counties which were to be settled under the plantation
scheme: Armagh, Cavan, Donegal, Fermanagh, Londonderry and
Tyrone. In the case of Londonderry most of these settlers were still
clustered around the two main ports of entry, Derry and Coleraine.
Such movement as had taken place was southward down the Foyle
valley to Strabane rather than into the heart of the county itself.
Although the numbers of settlers increased rapidly, so that by 1619
there were between 6,100 and 6,400 adult males in the planted
counties, they were still in a minority by comparison to the native Irish
and the threat of a native uprising was ever present.[15]

The presence of woodkern, the bandits of Gaelic Ireland, was a
perennial one. As Thomas Blennerhasset had written in his *A Direc-
tion for the Plantation in Ulster*, published in London during 1610, 'yet
the cruel woodkern, the devouring wolf and other suspicious Irish
would so attend on their [the settlers'] business, as their being there
should be little profitable unto them' and 'for although there be no
apparent enemy, nor any visible main force yet the woodkern and
many other (who now have put on the smiling countenance of content-
ment) do threaten every hour, if opportunity of time and place doth
serve to burn and steal whatsoever'. Such was this fear that in the
Londonderry settlement men refused to work alone in the woods.[16]

While the undertakers certainly feared the woodkern they were
nevertheless reluctant to take any action which might have protected
themselves. The *Orders and Conditions* of the Ulster Plantation, the
rules under which the settlers were to operate, had required them to
live together in villages and build fortified enclosures, castles and
bawnes, for their protection. However, as the various reports on the
development of the plantation scheme were made, including one in
early 1615, it became clear that the settlers were not fulfilling their
obligations. In 1615 many settlers had only recently arrived to take up
their holdings while others had not yet come at all and there were fears
in some quarters of another rebellion on the scale of the recently ended
Nine Year's War, the ruins of which were still visible in the landscape,

which would undo the whole scheme. The plantation had not been established long enough to encourage settlers to invest in substantial buildings. Many, in Chichester's words, were 'labouring rather for the most part to make profit of the lands than to erect strong buildings'.[17] Perhaps, although only newly arrived in Ulster, the environment in which they found themselves did not appear sufficiently strange to them to make them invest heavily in fortification, despite recurrent threat of attack.

The perennial inadequacy of security and persistent fear of rebellion was heightened in early 1615 by bad news from various sources. Trouble was brewing in the area which had traditionally been disturbing for Ulster – the western Isles of Scotland. The death of the old lord of the Isles, Angus Macdonnell of Dunyveg, in March 1614, had brought renewed warfare in the Isles. Previous experience indicated that such warfare usually spilled over into Antrim sooner or later. This was, however, different from earlier trouble in the area in that all the agreements which Angus had made with the government in Edinburgh were conveniently forgotten: this was not simply clan warfare it was full scale rebellion. Trouble dragged on intermittently into 1615 and 1616 and there were several military expeditions, including one from Ireland, which attempted to recover the castle of Dunyveg for the crown.[18]

Bad news also came from elsewhere. From continental Europe there was a growing amount of intelligence which indicated that the exiled earl of Tyrone was on the move in an attempt to invade Ireland. From Sir Dudley Carleton in Venice came news, in March 1614, that Tyrone was preparing to leave Rome and go to Flanders where he would marshal the Irish regiments serving with the Spanish forces there to invade Ireland. A few months earlier a priest had been seen in county Tyrone preaching that the English were heretics and that the pope wished the Catholic native community to go into rebellion. The Irish were to be of good courage as the earl of Tyrconnell was about to return at the head of 18,000 men supplied by the king of Spain and according to a prophecy in a book at Rome, conveniently unspecified, England had only two years to rule in Ireland. Further evidence of Tyrone's impending return was provided in March 1615 when James Meagh, a priest, arrived at Cork bringing news that the earl of Tyrone's invasion of Ireland was imminent.[19]

There was, in fact, some substance to these reports because Tyrone was petitioning to leave Rome and return to Ireland at the head of some sort of armed force. However, both the king of Spain and the pope were actively discouraging him from doing so. They feared such action would damage relations with James I with whom the king of Spain was negotiating a match between his daughter and James's son, the future Charles I. The Dublin administration, however, was not fully aware of the niceties of the politics of continental Europe. What it feared was an invasion. By early March 1615 Chichester was convinced that 'the hearts of the natives are against the state' and more soldiers were required to maintain law and order. The previous six months, he claimed, had seem a dramatic upsurge in cruel murders as the native Irish became more confident of Tyrone's return and the inevitable overthrow of the settlement of Ireland.[20] Dublin administrators expected a conspiracy and in April 1615 they found one. What they did not realise was that the plot they had uncovered did not quite measure up to the one they had expected to find.

2. The Plots

Over the ensuing three months, in the late spring and early summer of 1615, the outlines of the conspiracy discovered by Chichester in April became gradually clearer as the process of taking sworn statements, or depositions, from those who had any knowledge of the conspiracy proceeded. In order to frame a bill of indictment the administration needed a detailed knowledge of precisely who the conspirators were and what they had done. When Chichester wrote to the Privy Council in April 1615 informing them of the discovery of the conspiracy he had only the sketchiest of knowledge of what had gone on. His evidence depended on the depositions of two men, Tadhg O'Lennan, who was not a reliable witness by anyone's standard, and Dermot og O'Dunn. There were clearly problems with both confessions since they contained information which could not possibly be correct and the government knew it. At one point in O'Lennan's examination, for example, a marginal note that 'This is merely mistaken' was added. In O'Dunn's examination, for instance, a Franciscan friar called Edmond O'Mullarkey figured prominently; yet he was not in Ireland at this time. O'Mullarkey had been chaplain to Sir Cahir O'Doherty during his rebellion of 1608 but following the defeat of O'Doherty in July 1608 O'Mullarkey had fled to Spain, and by 1612 he was in Rome. Apart from a brief period when he acted as an army chaplain to the Irish forces in Flanders it appears he remained in Rome until his death in 1627.[21] His inclusion in some of the early depositions of 1615 might have appeared plausible because of his earlier connection with O'Doherty but his whereabouts were known by the administration. He was therefore quickly dismissed as a suspect and was not included in the list of conspirators drawn up in early May 1615 by the solicitor general.[22] Similarly those who used the conspiracy as a cover to settle local scores by making unwarranted accusations had to be weeded out. Knogher Mac Gilpatrick O'Mullen, for example, deposed that Art Mac Tomlin O'Mullin had made accusations against Brian Mac Shane O'Mullan during a row between them. Both parties admitted that there had been an argument between them but denied the accusation of involvement in the plot. Brian was never charged with conspiracy.

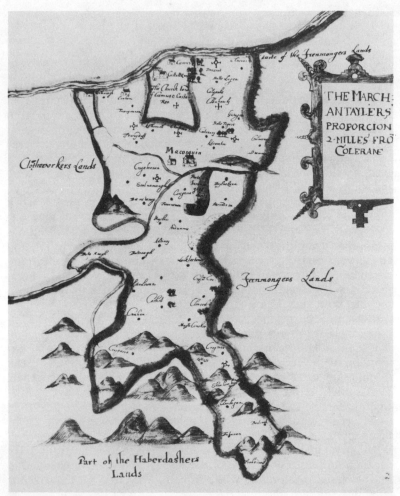

The Merchant Tailors' estate in c. 1622 by Thomas Raven. The River Bann runs along the top of the estate and 'Donerat', Nicholas Gill's freehold, is at the top right.

From the collection of depositions the outline of the conspiracy began to take shape. It began probably in late May 1614 in the house of Nicholas Gill in the part of the townland of Donerat known as Moyhullagh, now in the parish of Macosquin, on the banks of the river Bann, about three miles south of Coleraine. Gill had come to the town of Coleraine as a small merchant and had acquired the freehold of the sixty acres of Donerat from the Merchant Tailors in whose proportion it lay. On this land he built a house of timber.[23] He seems to have established himself as an alehouse keeper there since, in late May, Rory O'Cahan, Alexander Macdonnell, his uncle Loder and his brother Sorley Macdonnell, Rice Macdonnell, James og Mac Henry, Gorie Gilpatrick Mac Gorie Mac Henry, James Mac Brian O'Mullan, Shane MacGilladuff og O'Mullan, Art Mac James O'Mullan and Gorey Mac Manus O'Cahan were all at the house drinking beer. Alexander and Rory were both in foul mood. Over the previous two months, Alexander had had a series of frustrating meetings with his uncle, Sir Randal MacDonnell, about his rights to certain lands, which, as we shall see later, Alexander considered to be his own. He had recently been with his uncle at a meeting with the brother of the earl of Abercorn who was involved in a scheme of Sir Randal's to have a private act passed in the 1615 parliament which would deny Alexander any interest in Sir Randal's lands until all Sir Randal's children were provided for.[24] Rory was also frustrated about the breakup of his father's lands as part of the plantation scheme and his allocation of land in recompense.

In this frame of mind, no doubt encouraged by the beer, they planned to seize the towns of Derry, Coleraine, Lifford, Culmore and Limavady. In addition, Rory wanted to decapitate Sir Thomas Phillips whom he considered had cheated his family out of their rights! It was intended that the rebellion would take place in August 1615 and that in the intervening fifteen months the conspirators would organize themselves. Alexander Macdonnell promised to organise the forces from north Antrim and to approach Collo MacGillenaspig, one of the dispossessed Macdonnells from the Isles who had been caught up in the rebellion there, to assist them. Rory was to concentrate on the local native Irish gentry although his dynamism was rather lacking as in June 1615 he had still not got as far as approaching them.

One concrete action was undertaken. Fearing a repeat of the O'Doherty rebellion in 1608, which had been defeated because the full English military power was brought to bear on a rising which spread no further than the borders of counties Donegal and Londonderry, measures were taken to diversify the geography of the plot. A letter was sent to a number of minor native Irish gentry including Art og Mac Donnell O'Neill and Brian Crossagh O'Neill, a cousin, albeit illegitimate, of the earl of Tyrone, asking if they would manage the rebellion in the south-west of the province. Their responsibilities would include the burning of Mountjoy, Dungannon, and Charlemount and the release of Tyrone's son Con who was held in Charlemount. It is not clear why these men were selected. In the case of Art og O'Neill and his brother Owen the choice appears to have been a strange one as they had remained loyal to the Dublin government during O'Doherty's rebellion and were rewarded with pensions in 1610.[25] Possibly personal friendships played a part here.

The letters were prepared by one of those present who could write, Shane Mac Gilladuff O'Mullan, and delivered by a dwarf, Dalton Duff, who was a servant of Alexander Macdonnell. When Duff arrived at Brian Crossagh's he read the letter to him. Brian was apparently illiterate. Such fundamental difficulties in communication were common in native Irish society. Illiteracy was usual, even among the greater lords, since society was based primarily not on written documents, but on oral tradition as preserved by the hereditary literary classes such as the poets, historians and lawyers. A man's place in society, for example, was determined by his genealogy, manufactured or otherwise, rather than by what written contracts he had entered into.[26] In this case what is surprising is not that Brian Crossagh was illiterate but that one of the plotters could read and write and that the servant who was also a dwarf could at least read.

The evidence of the reaction to these letters is mixed. Art og apparently agreed to enter into the conspiracy and wrote in English to Macdonnell but Brian, by his own admission, was at this stage cautious. Brian Crossagh considered that the plot had little hope of success and for that reason was reluctant to be involved. In August, another letter was sent to Brian by Cuconnacht O'Keenan who read the letter for Brian. This letter seems to have fulfilled Brian's condition that there should be Scottish aid for the plot. Brian later denied that he agreed there and then, which may be true, but he became deeply implicated within a few weeks as he began to recruit new activists. A number of things had happened in late August 1614 to change his mind, including an unfortunate incident at the Tyrone assize at Dungannon which we shall examine later. He approached a number of people including Dermot og O'Dunn who was later to expose the conspiracy and Brian may have attempted to recruit some Maguires from Fermanagh to whom he was distantly related by marriage. As far as we know Macdonnell and O'Neill did not meet at this time and the letters which passed between them were, according to the later depositions, vague promises rather than plans for concerted action.

At this stage there does not seem to have even been a coherent plan. Only one deponent, Tadhg O'Lennan gave any indication of a detailed

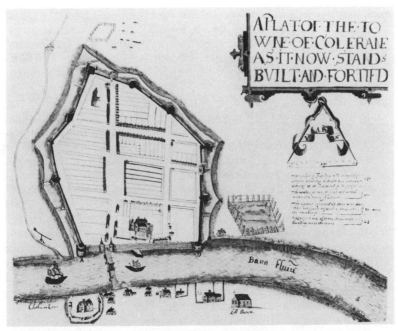

The town of Coleraine in c. 1622 by Thomas Raven.

plan. According to his story, Rory and some others were to go to a
tavern in Coleraine and drink there for the day. After the gates had
closed they would open them again. The rebels would storm in and
take the town, massacring everyone except Tristram Berrisford, the
Londoner's former agent, and their present agent, John Rowley,
whom they would use as hostages for bargaining. They could then go
on to take – by unspecified methods – Derry, Lifford, Massarine,
Carrickfergus and Mountjoy.

Such a plot would have conformed to the stereotype of contemporary conspiracies: the reference to the alehouse, for example, would
have confirmed all contemporary beliefs about the sort of iniquities
carried on there. The London Companies had sought to limit the
number of alehouses in Coleraine and Derry because, as they
explained to their agent, John Rowley, in 1612, 'having [been] credibly
informed and in our experience know that by the great number of
tavern and alehouses much disorder is committed and the poorer sort
spend their time and substance'. Sir Thomas Phillips wanted to go one
stage further in 1623 when he argued that all alehouses in remote
places should be banned as dens of iniquity.[27] Yet more violent were
the comments of the anonymous Old English author of the *Adver-*

tisements for Ireland, composed about 1623, who noted that the ruin of all countries were the things which 'introduce pride, prodigality, riot and all other monsters of excess'. The worst of these was 'quaffing and gluttony used in taverns and other places of that kind there which being the root of all vice and bestiality' and changed men into 'no other than brute animals'.[28] These views were not simply those of a minority. The administration had planned to introduce a bill into the 1613-15 parliament which would suppress alehouses and encourage inns, which provided lodging for travellers. Political difficulties in that parliament meant that it was not introduced but an administrative system for licensing alehouses was introduced instead. An alehouse keeper was required to have a licence costing ten shillings a year. Such a licence would be granted only on the recommendation of the justices of the peace at the Quarter Sessions.[29]

If the plan to take Coleraine and Derry as revealed by O'Lennan was not the invention of his fertile imagination then it had a number of drawbacks. The most serious handicap was its proposed execution with the six swords and one gun, purchased from a discontented soldier, which comprised the rebels' arms stockpile a few weeks before the rising was to begin. It may be, as Gorie MacManus O'Cahan suggested in his deposition, that they hoped to acquire arms from the houses they seized. However, if this were the case they were likely to be disappointed. Although the Orders and Conditions for the plantation scheme specified that undertakers were to hold in their houses 'at all times a convenient store of arms', to supply their tenants in the event of a rising, this was more honoured in the breach than the observance. An undertaker with 2,000 acres was to have at least twelve muskets and twelve calivers for every twenty-four tenants but when George Alleyne, the muster master general, examined the stores of arms in 1619 he found 230 muskets, 417 calivers and 1,141 swords among the 2,000 men mustered in Ulster. County Londonderry was not one of the better armed areas with one sword for every two men and one musket for every six.[30]

Following the frantic activity of the summer of 1614 the plot seems almost to have died. Heavy frost and snow during the winter of 1614-15 made travel and communications difficult and none of the deponents mention any specific activity connected with the planned rising through the winter. The discontents which gave rise to the plot in the first place did not, however, go away. According to the deposition of Cahal O'Hara, a mid-Antrim landowner and a tenant of Sir Randal Macdonnell, there had been an acrimonious interview between Sir Randal and his nephew, Alexander, just after Christmas during which Sir Randal had again refused his nephew some land which he had earlier promised him.

In early January there was evidence that Rory O'Cahan's feelings had not subsided when he arrived at the house of Manus Mac Gilreagh O'Mullan accompanied by a number of the O'Doherty's from Innishowen and a number of others all armed. Manus was not on the best of terms with Rory. He was friendly with Sir Thomas Phillips and he was also detaining some of Rory's father's cattle. Rory was probably drunk on the occasion and he demanded more drink. Manus's son Donnell, who was entertaining some of Sir Thomas Phillip's men at the time, refused. Rory accused Donnell of caring more for Sir Thomas than for him and hinted darkly that in the near future he might be in a position to do more for Donnell than could Sir Thomas. Rory was physically ejected and after some attempt to re-enter, he went away. He returned next day to apologise for his actions.

The plot seems to have come into life again in a half hearted way early in 1615. Shane Boy MacGillduff O'Mullan deposed that he had seen Alexander Macdonnell and Rory O'Cahan drinking together at Inishloughan during the early months of the year and that Macdonnell had given O'Cahan a target (a small shield) towards building up an cache of arms. Some of the plotters were, however, becoming restless. In late March two of the sons of Niall Mac Hugh O'Neill wrote to Alexander Macdonnell asking for more concrete evidence of intent than had been shown over the last year of talk. They sent the letter by 'a fool' to whom Macdonnell gave a coat when he arrived. The evidence for Macdonnell's reaction is confused. According to O'Lennan's deposition he instructed his clerk, Patrick Ballagh O'Murray, to write to Brian Crossagh O'Neill and to the others setting 10 May as the date for the rising. He chose a day when the gentry, who were also the military commanders, would be at parliament. O'Murray denied such a letter had ever been written, which is probably true. According to O'Lennan, Macdonnell wrote on Monday 3 April and sent the fool to deliver the letters. Yet the fool, still wearing the coat of Irish frieze, was arrested the following day with O'Lennan at Dramocke and he had no papers on him. A journey which would have meant virtually a circuit of the province could not have been achieved in under twenty-four hours, especially since he was lame.

O'Lennan was arrested on 4 April and according to the deposition of the soldier who arrested O'Lennan, Coll Duff Mac Quillan, he was prepared to bargain, offering to divulge a matter of great service to the king. He was seized by the provost marshal, Thomas Foster, and carefully questioned. The office of provost marshal was used extensively in the late sixteenth century, mainly in Ireland, to deal with disbanded soldiers, vagabonds and highway robbers by applying martial law to these people.[31] The officer was not widely loved, mainly because of the rigour with which he enforced his duties and on at least one occasion in 1616 Moses Hill, the provost marshal of Ulster had to be pardoned 'because in strictness of law he may be questioned for the execution of offenders by martial law'.[32] Some of the odium felt for these men was revealed in the demands of the Old English of the Pale for reforms in 1626, the Graces, number thirty-three of which demanded that the number of provosts marshal be limited to one for each county and their forces were to be subject to the same regulation as the army which in effect meant that the summary execution of martial law could no longer be used.[33] While the powers of the provost marshal were considerable they were regarded as necessary to meet the problems of early seventeenth century Ulster. High on the list of instructions from the king to the lord deputy in 1614 was to order the disarming of all suspicious persons who 'go around up and down the country in a disordered manner'. As many provosts marshal as were required were to be appointed to this task.

To fall into the hands of the provost marshal if one had a dubious reputation, as O'Lennan had, was a serious matter and usually meant summary execution. However one of Sir Thomas Phillips's own soldiers, Murtagh Mullan, reported to him that O'Lennan had been seized by the provost marshal and Phillips ordered that he be brought to him at Toome. O'Lennan, however, denied that he was prepared to do any deal and said he knew nothing. He was returned to the provost marshal and was apparently released. Two days later O'Lennan was rearrested as the implications were realised of other evidence coming to light. A deposition made to Edmond Blomer, the sheriff of Tyrone and later another deposition made on 3 April 1615 to George Montgomery, bishop of Meath, Toby Caulfield and Francis Annesley by Dermot og O'Dunn about the Brian Crossagh O'Neill dimension of the plot cast further suspicion on O'Lennan. The reasons for O'Dunn revealing the conspiracy at this time are not clear. On 9 April O'Lennan made a statement to the provost marshal of Londonderry setting out the Macdonnell side to the plot and three days later in another statement taken before Sir Thomas Phillips, he confirmed the substance of what O'Dunn had said to be true.

What followed was a complex process of collecting evidence and making arrests and attempting to tighten security in Ulster. The available evidence was not enough to secure convictions, especially against men with as much influence as Alexander Macdonnell. Indeed none of the Macdonnells had been arrested in mid-May when Robert Williamson, who had been taken prisoner by the Scottish pirate Collo Mac Gillenaspig, told of how he had been in a party of men earlier in the month on Rathlin when Collo had gone to meet Rory O'Cahan, Alexander Macdonnell and Sorley Macdonnell. What they discussed is not known but by that stage the conspiracy was over and Sorley

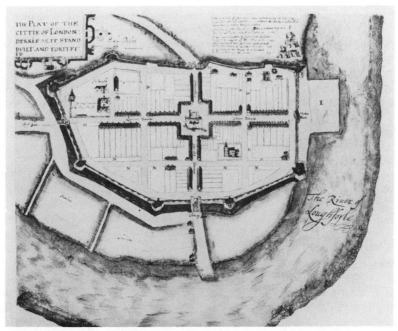

The city of Derry in c. 1622 by Thomas Raven.

together with 'twenty-four or twenty-five of the idle loose men of Sir
Randal's country' had already made their escape to the Scottish Isles
where they were to become part of the complicated rebellion going on
there.

The immediate problem which the administration tried to deal with
was that of security. The London Privy Council summoned before it
the Governor and Committee for the Londonderry plantation and
informed them of the plot, pointing out how vulnerable the towns of
Coleraine and Derry were to such plotting. It had been part of the
agreement between the crown and the Irish Society for the settlement
of Londonderry that the two towns would be walled and strongly
defended. However all this cost money and the Londoners who were
already making a loss on the venture had done little to fulfil these
conditions. An earthen wall had been erected around Coleraine but it
was already beginning to crumble and the walls around Derry,
although under construction by 1615, would not be completed for
another three years. In response to the Privy Council request the
Committee prevaricated. They asked for time to consider where a fort
might be built to protect the settlement and promised to give orders for
the further strengthening of Derry. On 1 May some concrete action

was taken. The Irish Society promised to raise money for arms from each of the twelve companies involved in the settlement which were to be sent to Derry and Coleraine for defence. On 10 July 1615 they fulfilled their promise when the *Seaflower* from the port of London docked at Coleraine carrying cargoes for a number of merchants and arms for the Londoners. The arms, valued at over £112, included 144 swords, 48 pikes, 1 musket, 6 barrels of gunpowder, 2 small cannon and light armour for 94 men. However all other promises faded away and, although the question of building a fort at Coleraine was raised at a meeting of the Common Council of the Irish Society in May, nothing was ever done.[34]

The second precaution immediately taken by the Privy Council was to remove the focus of some of the conspirators activity, Con O'Neill, the son of the exiled earl of Tyrone. When Tyrone left Ireland on 3 September 1607 his departure had been so rushed that he left his fourth son behind him. Con had been seized by the government and entrusted to the care of Sir Toby Caulfield. Caulfield was a distinguished soldier who had seen service on Martin Frobisher's expedition to the Azores in the 1580s and later in the Low Countries and at Cadiz before coming to Ireland to fight in the Nine Year's War. He was the commander of the fort at Charlemount, which he held on lease from the crown and was appointed receiver of Tyrone's estate when the earl fled in 1607. Con remained at Charlemount until May 1615 when, as a result of the plot, the Privy Council felt he should be sent where he would not be a rallying point for other malcontents . They ordered that he should attend Eton where he would be educated as an English gentleman. He left Dublin in June 1615 and was installed as a fellow commoner, the upper of the two ranks of commoners at Eton, where he remained until August 1622 when he was in his early twenties. In August he was committed to the Tower for reasons which are not known and nothing more is heard of him.[35]

After the immediate precautions of late April and early May 1615 there came the more long term problem of piecing together what had actually happened in the conspiracy so that arrests could be made and a case constructed against the conspirators. Over the period April to June more than thirty-three depositions were taken from various individuals and compared. The first group of depositions were taken before Thomas Phillips between 12 and 26 April. There was then an interlude and no more were taken until 10 May when another group of possible suspects were examined. Another gap then followed until 27 May by which time the main conspirators had been arrested and examined; Loder Macdonnell on 29 May and Brian Crossagh on 31 May. After this the prisoners were moved to Dublin where they were examined further in late June before being returned to Derry for trial at the assize in early July.

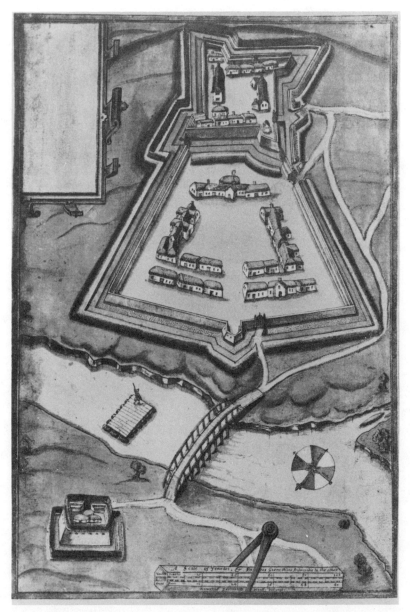

Charlemount Fort by Richard Bartlett, 1602. The basic design remained unchanged while Con O'Neill was held here. It was rebuilt in the 1620s.

The removal to Dublin at least resolved one problem of the local administration: that of security. Initially some of the prisoners, including Rory O'Cahan and James og Mac Henry, were imprisoned in the house of a local man, James Powsher, and guarded by two soldiers. There was at least one attempt to bribe the soldiers with money and drink but to no avail. Shortly after this the prisoners were moved to the county gaol at Derry but the attempts at bribery did not cease. Intercessions were also made on behalf of some of the conspirators by their families. In late April 1615 Honora Ni Gilligan, wife to James Mac Brian O'Mullan came to the settler Anthony Mahue, her 'gossip' or friend, in an attempt to persuade Anthony to intercede with Sir Thomas Phillips on behalf of her husband who, she claimed, had been enticed into the conspiracy against his wife's advice and was kept there by force. She offered Anthony a cow for his trouble and a bribe of twenty cows for Phillips.

The task of taking the examinations and establishing some order within the stories told by the plotters was unusually difficult. On some occasions interpreters had to be used since the deponents spoke only Irish. George Sexton, Chichester's secretary, acted as interpreter for Gorie Mac Manus O'Cahan's deposition and for that of Cuconnacht O'Keenan. One Davie O'Mullan was also described as an interpreter and George Cornwall and Thomas Wall were interpreters for one deposition taken in late June before Toby Caulfield at Charlemount to ascertain the involvement of the Maguires in the plot. One of the accused, Patrick Ballagh O'Murray, Alexander Macdonnell's secretary, even acted as interpreter on one occasion although only with George Sexton also present.

A second problem which emerged as some of the depositions were taken was that at least some of the conspirators had tried to agree a common story between them. However, this seems to have broken down quickly as one informed on another hoping for preferential treatment. Some of the accused tried to blackmail each other into exonerating them. Brian Crossagh O'Neill, for instance, threatened to reveal O'Keenan as a horse thief if he implicated him. Gradually, however, the picture began to emerge and by the end of June the Dublin administration felt sufficiently confident of being able to go to trial at the summer assizes at Derry which were to be held in July.

3. The Plotters

The depositions taken by the Dublin administration were for the construction of a case against the plotters which was to be set out in a bill of indictment which would be presented to the grand jury before the trial. The depositions were concerned with names, dates and places, and not directly with the motivation which drew the conspirators together. For an explanation of why rather than how we must turn to other sources to piece together the grievances and attitudes of the plotters. It was the assumption of both contemporaries and those who, for varying reasons which we shall look at later, were later to write about the lives of the plotters that the plot was a reaction to the redistribution of lands under the plantation scheme in Ulster. Yet few of the leaders of the conspiracy had been affected by that scheme. The key figures in the plot were Scots Macdonnells and the central figure on the native Irish side was Brian Crossagh O'Neill who had received a substantial grant of lands in north east Tyrone as part of the plantation. Most of the available evidence suggests that despite the fears of the Dublin government the plantation scheme did not provoke widespread hostility among the Ulster Irish. There was some initial dissatisfaction with the plantation arrangements but this does not seem to have developed into a more coherent movement and had melted away by 1616. Indeed many native Irish poets, for example, saw the flight of the earls in September 1607 not as a defeat imposed by the English but as self-inflicted punishment from God for the arrogance of the great lords. Some were prepared to accept James I as the new 'high king' and to stitch him into the social order of Ireland with an appropriate genealogy and praise poetry in his honour as they had done with new lords for generations.[36] One such poet, Eoghan Ruadh Mac an Bhaird, lamenting the imprisonment of Niall Garbh O'Donnell, the brother of two of the conspirators, did not blame the English for the imprisonment but rather saw an appeal to the king as Niall's best chance of release.[37] What the poets lamented in the years after the flight was the disappearance of the patronage on which they had depended rather than the abstract concept of a disappearing 'Gaelic Ireland'. In general, the falling status of the poets in the new order was all too obvious.

Cuconnacht O'Keenan's brother Tadhg, for example, had been one of the poets attached to the Maguires. He fled to Rome with Maguire and the other earls in September 1607 and later composed an account of his adventures in Europe. When he left Ireland he had owned fourteen cows, eight calves, two horses and twenty-five pigs valued in total at an impressive £22 6s. 2d. By the time of the conspiracy, Cuconnacht, described as 'a rhymer or chronicler belonging to Connor Roe Maguire', was reduced to begging from Loder MacDonnell who gave him ten shillings 'for a help' and promised him a cow.[38]

The poets reacted to changing circumstances in many different ways. Some, such as the Fermanagh poet Eochaidh O hEodhusa and the Donegal chronicler Lughaidh Ó Cléirigh, accepted lands as part of the plantation scheme and some continued as poets within the new order, especially where the survivors of the old families continued to patronise them. Another of Cuconnacht's brothers, Brian og, was involved in Brian Maguire's attempt in the 1630s to gather together and transcribe the old histories of Ireland, such as the *Leabhar Gabhála*. Other poets were also patronised by new settler landlords.[39] This was not a new development. In the years before 1607 Eoghan Ruadh Mac an Bhaird, for example, was equally adept at wishing Turlough O'Neill, grandson of Turlough Luineach O'Neill, success in his negotiations with the London administration over a land deal and urging others to go into rebellion against that administration.[40] Others, such as Fearghal og Mac an Bhaird, seeing no future in Ireland went to Scotland where an older order still survived, or to the continent to become clergy or scribes to patrons there. In this they were continuing an old tradition since sons of the literati had been clergy for many generations.

All of this is not to argue that there were not genuine grievances resulting from the imposition of a new order on Ulster. Rory O'Cahan, son of Sir Donnell O'Cahan, and Donnell Mac Con O'Donnell and Hugh Boy Mac Con O'Donnell, brothers of Sir Niall Garbh O'Donnell, had every reason to be aggrieved since their father and brother respectively had been imprisoned without trial in the Tower of London for almost six years. Sir Donell O'Cahan, a son in law of the earl of Tyrone, had from the outbreak of the Nine Year's War in 1594 been trying to manipulate the situation to his own advantage. Initially he had sided with Tyrone but with the arrival of English forces under Sir Henry Dowcra at Derry in 1600 he made a swift change of side on condition that he should have a grant of all the O'Cahan lands.[41]

As chief of the O'Cahan's, under native Irish arrangements, Donnell would not have owned the clan lands. Rather he would simply have exercised lordship over them with the freeholders paying him a token rent. The more freeholders he could persuade to defect from another lord and rely on him for protection, the greater his status would be. The *Annals of Connacht* demonstrated the point by admitting the exception of one of his ancestors in 1524, 'Cu Maige Ballagh son of Domhnaill O'Cahan, who was, considering [the fewness of] his followers the best gentleman of his race'. O'Cahan was in turn sub-lord to O'Neill. He paid to O'Neill each year twenty-one beeves and money from every quarter of land as well as entertainment and was obliged to supply men for a hosting.[42]

A grant of lands on the English model would not only have made O'Cahan a substantial landowner but would also have eliminated O'Neill's influence over those lands. As the war went against O'Neill it seemed that this might come about since in 1602 O'Cahan was granted the custody of his country. However, with the conclusion of peace in 1603 and the regranting to O'Neill of the lands over which he had exercised lordship before the war O'Cahan's grant was quietly forgotten by all but O'Cahan.

For the next four years he took cases against the earl of Tyrone to various courts in an attempt to force a separate grant of his lands to be made to him. In this he had the support of various government officials, including Sir John Davies, the attorney general, who were convinced that the grant made to the earl of Tyrone was overgenerous and should be curtailed.[43] With Tyrone's flight to the continent, in which the harassment by O'Cahan had played no small part, O'Cahan recognised that his bargaining power was gone. He feared that his land would be redistributed among other branches of the sept as had been done with the MacMahon lands in Monaghan and the O'Reilly land in Cavan. He became increasingly insolent to royal officials in the vicinity of his estates and refused to obey royal warrants. Lord Deputy Chichester, fearing that he would cause trouble, had him arrested by Sir Thomas Phillips in February 1608. Once arrested neither Chichester nor the Privy Council had any idea how to proceed. Despite general accusations of treason they had little firm evidence against him save that he was a troublemaker. In July 1609 he was sent to the Tower of London where he stayed until he died in 1628.[44]

The case of Niall Garbh O'Donnell was less complex. Like O'Cahan he had used the Nine Year's War to make a bid for power against the main family of O'Donnell and had joined Sir Henry Dowcra when he landed at Derry with the English forces in 1600. Again like O'Cahan his efforts had gone wrong since the main O'Donnell line was restored to the lands of Donegal as earls of Tyrconnell in 1603. In April 1608 Sir Cahir O'Doherty, insulted by his treatment at the hands of the governor of Derry, rose in rebellion. Within three months the rising had been suppressed but Niall Garbh O'Donnell had been implicated in the conspiracy, although probably wrongly so, by a letter written by

Inghean Dubh, the earl of Tyrconnell's mother. Niall, his son and the
two brothers who were later among the conspirators were arrested in
June 1608. No criminal offence could be found against Niall's brothers and they were released on security of good behaviour. Niall was
tried in the court of king's bench in Dublin in June 1609. The trial
lasted eight or nine hours but the jury failed to agree. Despite
inducements to the jury to find O'Donnell guilty, including an enforced three day fast, they would not do so. Niall Garbh shared the same
fate as O'Cahan – he was sent to the Tower were he died in 1625.[45]
Imprisonment in the Tower was not a sign of ignominy, rather the
reverse. It was a recognition of their nobility. A list of the prisoners in
the Tower in 1612 included one pretender to the throne, Lady
Arabella Stuart, four peers, including the earl of Northumberland
and the Countess of Shrewsbury, and a number of knights, the most
prominent being Sir Walter Raleigh.[46] Their style of living was also
fairly good as when in 1621 the administration made a grant towards
their maintenance they received almost three times what a normal
prisoner was allowed.[47]

Thus the relatives of O'Cahan and O'Donnell had just cause to be
aggrieved. They had yet further cause. While the two men were
imprisoned in the Tower other members of the family could not gain
control of their lands. Moreover, as was normal in the early seventeenth century, the families had to pay for the prisoners' keep in the
Tower. This soon proved to be too much of a drain on the family
resources and in 1621 the government had to make them an allowance
to support the prisoners. Furthermore, in the absence of the landhol-
ders, the estates and the economic fortunes of the families began to
decline. Some were already in debt for various reasons. In 1610
O'Cahan had mortgaged a large block of land and the fishing rights of
Faughan to a Dublin merchant and land speculator, Nicholas Weston.
He had been having difficulties even before this. O'Cahan had leased
most of his lands from the managers of the earl of Tyrone's estate
after his flight for £330 a year. By 1608 all that had been paid of this
was £130 which had been taken by distraint and the balance of £200
had been paid by a mortgage on the land.[48]

O'Donnell was in no better shape. Of the land he leased from
O'Neill for £100 only £35 was paid and in 1612 one Patrick Conley
petitioned Lord Salisbury that Niall owed him £1,314 6s. 6d., on a
mortgage of land. Sir Donnell O'Cahan had also been unfortunate
since he had entrusted one Rice Gilmore to manage his estate during
his absence and had given him a considerable sum of money to do
this. Gilmore had not only embezzled the money but had also managed to obtain title for himself to some of O'Cahan's best land.[49]

A second problem was emerging for O'Cahan and O'Donnell. As

Chichester pointed out in 1608 when discussing O'Cahan and O'Donnell's poverty

> It may seem strange that those men who were accounted so great
> . . . should have no better revenues; but it may be answered that
> their maintenance is not from the money they receive but from
> their provisions of meat, butter, cuttings and cosherings which
> none of the people will afford to them or for their use whilst they
> are in prison or absent from their countries.[50]

Both Niall Garbh and Sir Donnell complained to the earl of Northampton, the king's principal secretary of state, and others of their inability to defend themselves against 'wicked tenants' who refused to pay their 'commyns' to the lord. It had been the practice for the great lords of Gaelic Ulster to let out some of their cattle, which was their main source of wealth, to their followers for pasturage which would be repaid at some future date – the practice of commyns – but with the absence of the lords many followers simply retained the cattle.[51]

In the early years of the seventeenth century the estates of these great lords were still being run on the lines of native Irish lordships, in which status was more important than property or profit. This system contrasted strongly with the more commercial aims which the new settlers were pursuing. Some native lords were still depending on the traditional nominal renders of followers rather than more commercially determined rents on settler estates. Hence the income of these men fell far behind the expenditure which they incurred and indebtedness followed. They mortgaged land in an attempt to fund their expenditure but without a radical overhaul of the 'recalcitrant tenants' the problem was insoluble. In sixteenth century Gaelic Ulster a lord of sufficient strength would attempt to exercise strong controls over his followers. Since the population was low and tenants were in short supply lords tried to hold those they had as followers by force if necessary. Thus in 1601 Niall Garbh could inform Sir Henry Dowcra that Innishowen was his country and 'I will cess my people...upon the churls, I will take such things as I want and employ the inhabitants at mine own discretion.... and for the people they are my subjects. I will punish, exact, cut, and hang, if I see occasion, where and whensoever I list'.[52] In the new environment of the seventeenth century with the common law acting as a counterweight to the powers of lords such controls were effectively ended. The 'warlords' of the sixteenth century were forced into the mould of landlords. Failure to accept their new role led to exile in the case of the earl of Tyrone or imprisonment as in the case of O'Cahan. It made estate management more difficult than it had been. Attempts to raise rents resulted in refusals to pay and desertions to other lords who were prepared to offer better terms. Land was abundant and labour scarce and the weakest landlords suffered most.

The result was that many of the native Irish who had been granted freeholds in Londonderry in the years before the conspiracy were forced to sell as a result of rising debt. By 1639 there were as many British as Irish in possession of native freeholds in the county.[53] It is, therefore, probably no coincidence that at least two of the conspirators, Gorie Mac Manus O'Cahan and Shane Mac Manus O'Cahan, were the sons of these early freeholders. They may well have seen no future for themselves within the system and in Gorie's case, at least, his fears were well justified since by the mid-1640s the family freeholding had already been in the hands of the settler family of Berrisford for some time.

The experience of Sir Donnell's sons and Niall Garbh's brothers in the years before the conspiracy was that of downward social mobility. Sir Donnell's bid for power in the early years of the century had gone badly wrong. Subsequently as part of the Ulster plantation scheme, ten per cent of the old the family lands, now the new county of Londonderry, was set aside for thirteen freeholds of varying size, totalling about 52,000 acres. Sir Donnell's sons had not come out of this process particularly well since they and their mother had received only 1,000 acres between them. It was their uncle, Manus O'Cahan, who had profited most from the carve up, receiving 2,000 acres for himself. Manus was not noted for his family loyalty. He had defected to the English during the Nine Year's War before his brother did so. In 1610 when Sir Donnell had written to him from the Tower asking him for help and warning him not to 'let covetous hope of land debar you from this' Manus had passed the letter to the lord deputy.[54]

The remainder of the O'Cahan lands in the newly created county of Londonderry were assigned to the London Companies who had undertaken to settle them. Some land was reserved for men who had settled in the area before the agreement with the Londoners. One such man was Sir Thomas Phillips, a professional soldier who had no gentry background. Aged about fifty at the time of the plot he had had extensive military experience in France, Spain, Portugal, Italy and Africa before coming to Ireland in the 1590s and had learnt to speak French and Spanish.[55] None of these accomplishments counted for much in the eyes of native Irishmen who had an exaggerated regard for genealogy and would have considered Phillips an upstart since he was not drawn from a landed family. Rory O'Cahan, son of Sir Donnell and one of the key conspirators, was intensely concerned with his status and that of his followers. Several deponents, including Charles

Fisher and Rice Jones, mentioned that during an argument between Rory O'Cahan and Daniel O'Mullan Rory accused Daniel of giving great respect to Sir Thomas Phillips's churls while making little of Rory's men. In the case of Phillips what rankled even more was the fact that he had been granted the old O'Cahan castle at Limavady and, as O'Keenan was later to depose, part of the plot may well have been an attempt to reclaim the Limavady castle. It is clear that such a social decline grated on Rory O'Cahan.

In some ways one might expect the story of Brian Crossagh O'Neill to be similar to that of the O'Cahans and O'Donnells. He was the illegitimate son of a brother of the earl of Tyrone, Cormac Mac Baron O'Neill who, like Sir Donnell O'Cahan and Niall Garbh O'Donnell, had been imprisoned in the Tower because of his associations with Tyrone. Brian's reaction to this situation was rather different to that of the others. Rather than declining in the social order Brian was rising. He would almost certainly not have done so under the old order since he had two elder brothers, Con and Art og. Following the flight of his

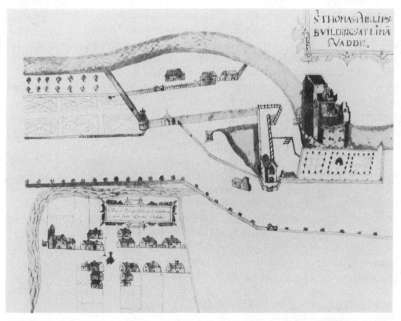

Sir Thomas Phillips' lands at Limavady c. 1622 by Thomas Raven. The O'Cahan castle is the heavily fortified building on the right. Phillips probably lived in the smaller building nearby. He also laid out the formal gardens. The village of Limavady, also built by Phillips, at the bottom left lay about a mile east of the castle.

uncle and the other Ulster lords, Brian was granted the rents of part of his uncle's lands in the parish of Kildress in north-east Tyrone, a grant which in 1611 was turned into a grant of 1,000 acres as part of the Ulster plantation scheme. The grant was not entirely altruistic since Sir Toby Caulfield, the administrator of O'Neill's lands following the flight pointed out that Brian was 'a young man very like to have joined O'Doherty, who by his birth and estimation was able to draw a great many idle followers after him to commit villainy and therefore he [Caulfield] had bestowed on him, the better to content him, the rents of one ballybetagh which yielded him £40 per annum'.[56]

In some ways Brian was not untypical of one group of native Irish under the plantation scheme. The removal of the top layer of the old order and the introduction of new settlers speeded up social mobility dramatically. With the removal of many of the older lineages, collateral branches of old families, such as Connor Maguire and the O'Neills of the Fews came to prominence with grants of lands under the new order. At a lower social level many settler landlords were more than content to lease considerable tracts of land to natives either because no suitable settler tenants were available or because the native Irish were prepared to pay higher rents. On the estate of Sir Claud Hamilton around Gortin in north Tyrone, for example, one native Irishman, Patrick Groome O'Dufferne, managed to become the middleman for the entire estate, subletting it to both natives and settlers, within three years of the beginning of the plantation scheme.[57] Such rapid mobility was also a source of some concern to the poets of Gaelic Ireland who saw their traditional patrons replaced by what they regarded upstarts and bitter complaint followed.[58]

Brian O'Neill's attitude to his new found wealth was one of speculation rather than consolidation. He seems to have done little with his new estate since it was commented in 1613 that he had only dug a small trench of earth of which he had built a small wall around his house but 'his land being no otherwise estated than before'. In 1612 when, as a result of changes in the border of county Tyrone, it was believed that his land now lay in Londonderry he attempted to sell it to the Irish Society, the governing body for the Londonderry settlement, and to 'demand great sums of money' for it. The Londoners responded by demanding that his grant be cancelled but the whole affair was proved on investigation to be a false alarm, the land having always been in county Tyrone.[59]

One reason why Brian may have been keen to sell was a growing realisation that his newfound temporal wealth did not mean that he was socially acceptable to the new gentry of Tyrone. According to O'Dunn's deposition during the assizes at Dungannon in 1614, which was one of the highpoints in the county gentry's social calendar, Brian was snubbed by the assize judges from Dublin and one of them, an Old English judge, Justice Aungier, 'was ready to revile me like a churl'. It was not simply the fact that he was a Gaelic Irishman that mattered, since many others who made the transition from one order to another were accepted as gentry, but rather the fact that he was an illegitimate son of a minor gentleman who had risen too fast for his own good. Aungier was not alone in his disapproval of such developments since it is a theme which runs through much of the native Irish poetry of the period. In Brian's case the insult was strongly felt.

The central figures in the conspiracy were not, however, native Irish with grievances about the new order but rather Scots Macdonnells. The conspiracy itself was initiated by Alexander Mac Sorley Macdonnell, a nephew of Sir Randal Macdonnell, later earl of Antrim, and the largest landowner in county Antrim. There is little doubt as to Alexander's motivation in initiating the plot – discontent with his uncle. He spelt out this resentment on more than one occasion. Patrick Ballagh O'Murray deposed that he had often heard Alexander voice his anger with his uncle because Sir Randal would not give him any land. In 1614 he had laid down an ultimatum to his uncle threatening that if he would not give him land he would get it in other ways. The origins of this grievance are to be found in the way in which Sir Randal had acquired the lands of north Antrim in the early seventeenth century.

Randal's claim to the lands he held was doubtful. The Glens of Antrim, as the result of a fifteenth-century marriage agreement, were the inheritance of the Dunyveg branch of the Macdonnell family. This had, by the 1590s, been seized from Angus Macdonnell, the rightful claimant, by his cousin James who was Sir Randal's brother and Alexander's father. James had also held the rest of north Antrim by inheritance from his own father Sorley Boy. When James died in 1601 the lands should have passed to Alexander's elder brother who died shortly after his father. However, Randal, James's younger brother, had by rather dubious means persuaded the crown to grant all the land to him. It is not difficult to imagine why Alexander was annoyed with his uncle who refused even to lease to him part of his rightful inheritance. Alexander, however, was an adventurer and not beyond using strong arm tactics when necessary. In 1624, for instance, he acquired some Antrim land simply by occupying it with a force of 100 men and a rumour circulated that he would build this force up into a private army. The plot, for Alexander Macdonnell, was the expression of personal frustration.[60]

Two other Macdonnells were also leading figures in the conspiracy: Loder and Sorley. Of Loder little is known save that he was a brother of Sir Randal, possibly illegitimate, and uncle to Alexander. Sorley, on the other hand, is a much more interesting figure. Sorley, a brother to Alexander, was a mercenary, prepared to fight on whichever side rewarded him best, his speciality being piracy. He was certainly involved in the rebellion by the Scottish Macdonnells during late 1614 and early 1615 in the Isles. Their hold on the lordship of the Isles was collapsing in the face of royal authority and they were also faced with the desire of the Campbells of Argyle to seize the lordship for themselves. Indeed, after the collapse of the Ulster conspiracy Sorley returned to Scotland although the rewards were poor and after a further brief sojourn in Antrim early in 1616 he headed for greener pastures. He seized one of Sir Thomas Phillips's ships on the Irish sea in 1616 and operated there as a pirate before seizing another ship, and after capturing a French ship he made for the haven of all seventeenth century pirates, Dunkirk. There he joined the Irish regiment serving in Flanders where he commanded a company for some years. In 1624 he saw some action in Bohemia and at Prague before returning to the Irish forces in the Spanish Netherlands. He never returned to Ireland although his son did go to Antrim to fight during the war of the 1640s.[61]

An interesting insight into Sorley's mind is provided by the compilations of Irish poetry and prose which he commissioned while in the Netherlands in the late 1620s. It is difficult to understand why a Scotsman should have commissioned such works. Certainly there was considerable cultural similarity between the Isles and Ulster so the works would not have been entirely foreign to him. Unfortunately we do not know whether or not Sorley was literate or whether or not he understood Irish, especially the formal language of the classically trained poets. Certainly his uncle Loder could not read Irish, although he could read English, and he employed a number of translators including Tadhg O'Lennan to deal with business involving his tenants which required the use of Irish. One reason for Sorley's commissioning of the works may well have been the simple act of patronage itself which would have been expected of a gentleman of Sorley's standing, and some of the marginal notes by the scribes on one of the documents are in praise of Sorley as a patron. This may explain, in part, why the texts, with one exception, *Duanaire Finn*, are seemingly random collections of poetry and a twelfth century text, the *Agallamh na Senorach*, which must have had little relevance to the life of a pirate turned army captain. Indeed there is some doubt as to whether Sorley actually ever took possession of the texts and at least one found its way into the Irish college at Louvain and was owned by the Franciscan John Colgan in 1658. One of the texts, the *Duanaire Finn* a collection of the stories of the fianna which were common to both Ireland and Scotland, may suggest something of Sorley's attitude. They depict Fionn as an outsider, as a man on the margins of society and also as a warrior with a code of military ethics: perhaps in the same way as Sorley saw himself which might possibly explain why he was keen to own such a work.[62]

Below this handful of leaders there was a sizeable number of others involved or implicated in the conspiracy. Inevitably many of these men below the ranks of the gentry are shadowy figures and it is difficult to discern their motives for becoming involved in the plot. Some at least were drawn from what the Dublin administrators called 'woodkern' – the bandits of seventeenth century Ireland. They were those who lived in the marginal areas of Ulster, the mountains and woodlands and conducted periodic raids on settled areas for cattle and money. As Chichester was to describe them 'being poor and wanting the means to live or otherwise pressed with the conscience or guilt of capital offences committed had betaken their keepings and out of the woods and other places of strength did usually rob'. Such masterless men were not unique to early seventeenth century Irish society. There had been frequent complaint about their activities in the sixteenth century and similar complaints continued unabated into the eighteenth century. Attempts were made in the early seventeenth century to bring them within the social order by assigning them masters. This took the form of requiring landlords to keep registers of those living on their lands and requiring native Irish to give bonds for their loyalty. In this way they were given a social standing and responsibilities.[63]

It is questionable how much real damage they did. The gaol delivery rolls for Ulster for the years immediately before the conspiracy suggest that Ulster may well have been at least as peaceful as most counties in northern England. The gaol delivery rolls contain details of those who were sent for trial at the assize because their crimes were too serious to be dealt with at the county based quarter sessions. The records which have survived for Ulster can be compared with those of Northumberland, a county relatively isolated from central government and, like Ulster, sparcely populated. In the early seventeenth century the population of Northumberland was probably about half that of Ulster although little evidence survives to be dogmatic on the point. The number of crimes in 1614, for example, was about half the Ulster total of 102. Detected crime was also similar in composition. About three quarters of Northumberland crime was simple theft, mainly of animals, and in Ulster theft, again mainly of sheep, pigs, cattle and horses, made up about 77 per cent of the total. Murder also formed about the same proportion in both cases.[64] The activities of the woodkern may have been given some encouragement in the early seventeenth century with the rapid growth of markets and fairs in Ulster at which they could more easily than before dispose of their stolen goods for ready money.[65]

Various forces worked in Ulster to keep crime at bay. People afraid of attack from outside formed themselves into tight communities where family and neighbours were able to arbitrate in disputes. Landlords too were keen to play a part in controlling the boisterous elements in the community, particularly if it meant that royal officials charged with the maintenance of law and order, such as the sheriff or justice of the peace, could be kept out of the landlord's business. The clergy, both Protestant and Catholic, were also a powerful influence for stability and frequently acted as mediators. In Dermot O'Dunn's deposition, for example, a friar was the mediator when a dispute broke out between two of the plotters. Ulster sensitivities to violence in the early seventeenth century were more heightened than earlier or later because of the fear of rebellion and the weakness of the British settlement in Ulster. In one raid woodkern could easily steal four or five cattle which would be the entire wealth of a recently arrived settler and thus drive him into destitution. This fear was more acutely felt in the spring of 1615 because of the bad winter during which, according to one computation, a fifth of all the cattle in Ireland had died. As Chichester admitted in 1611, if even three or four settlers were killed by woodkern it would have discouraged enough settlers from coming to Ulster to set the plantation scheme back many years.[66]

Not surprisingly woodkern were a fruitful recruiting ground for any conspiracy which offered gain. The original list of conspirators contained Donnell Mac Owen Mac Donnell O'Neill 'a desperate kern' and eight others were also referred to as kern. Donnell's life of crime is well documented. He had been pardoned on at least three previous occasions, in 1611, 1612 and 1614, apparently for his activities as a woodkern. Art og O'Neill, one of the early and more enthusiastic recruits to the plot had also been pardoned for woodkern activities on at least two previous occasions.[67]

Another example of such activities is provided by the career of Hugh Mac Shane O'Neill. Hugh lived in the heavily wooded area of Glen-conkyne in south Londonderry and was 'well able to raise store of men'. In the months following O'Doherty's rebellion in 1608 he and his followers had acted as bounty hunters, capturing Shane Carragh O'Cahan, uncle to Hugh's fellow conspirator Rory O'Cahan, 'understanding the [lord] deputy had granted a free pardon to every one who should kill a rebel together with his goods they took the opportunity to enrich themselves'. He also managed to acquire land near Brian Crossagh O'Neill in the plantation scheme but he did not keep it for long.[68] Another example of a 'trimmer', although not as blatant, was Owen Mac Cawell, who was implicated in the plot but not deeply enough involved to be put on trial for his activities. He featured in the report of George Montgomery, the bishop of Derry, on the state of his lands in 1607. There Mac Cawell is described as a very learned man, especially in civil law, and able to use Latin and Irish. According to Montgomery, however, he was keen witted, artful and crooked. Montgomery, hoping to win him over, 'for I prefer a fawning dog to a barking one', granted him the archdeaconry of Derry and he received a freeholding in the Londonderry settlement. It is clear, however, that Mac Cawell was not a man to let any opportunity for advancement slip and preferred to back all the horses, cultivating his contacts among the conspirators but not becoming sufficiently implicated to be convicted.[69]

There were also other men involved in the conspiracy who if they were not active woodkern had some form of criminal record or were known to the Dublin administration as being dubious in their loyalty. Hugh O'Mergee, a plotter, and Brian Modder O'Cahan, a father of one of the conspirators, had both been accused in the court of castle chamber in 1609 of 'acquitting ...traitors contrary to the clear evidence that they had been in open rebellion'. By order of the court both had been fined £100, pilloried at Dublin and Derry and had had an ear cut off.[70] The father of another conspirator, Gilladuff O'Mullan, was also known in Dublin as he had been objected to as unreliable when mentioned as a possible juror for the trial of Sir Donnell O'Cahan in 1608.[71] One other rebel, Donnell og Mac Donnell Boy had also recently been brought to the attention of the Dublin government. Only a month before the discovery of the conspiracy one James Mac Farrdonnough Mac Bryan Carragh had tried to sell some rather stale information to the authorities about a plot which was allegedly being hatched and implicated Donnell. However, Chichester had dismissed the evidence and James remained unpaid.[72]

There were clearly different motivations which brought these various men together in the conspiracy of 1615. Some acted out of desperation, others wanted revenge, some profit, and others simply action. They were also of different origin: some Scots and some native Irish. What bound them together was that they all for varying reasons had been pushed out from the centre of the social stage, denied social recognition because they were younger sons, declining gentry, *nouveaux riches*, or criminals. Many felt they had nothing to lose by this course of action. If they succeeded in the rising they would be on the road to power, wealth and social acceptance. If they failed all was not lost since if they seized the earl of Tyrone's son they could always flee to the continent where they would be treated as heroes. As Dermot O'Dunn alleged, Brian O'Neill told him 'if our fortunes be to speed well you shall have good commands under us; if not we can all go to Spain with the boy [Con O'Neill] and be welcome'.

The plotters had also been pushed out of the social limelight for another reason, their religion, since all were Catholic. It is this religious element, although it is not stated explicitly in the depositions, which may account for a priest, Father O'Laverty, who was Alexander Macdonnell's chaplain, being involved in the plot. In the years after 1603 the power of the Dublin administration became increasingly strong in Ulster, and the activities undertaken there included the promotion of the Reformation. In Londonderry under Bishop Montgomery the Reformation had made considerable progress. A number of the Catholic clergy had conformed and were instituted into Anglican cures and yet more native Irish subsequently conformed and became Anglicans. The diocese also had a good supply of English and Scots Protestant clergy. It is clear that there were a considerable number of converts both real and nominal. The result was that both religious groups appeared evenly balanced to many contemporaries, while the Reformation appeared to be making progress.[73] In this finely balanced situation, where neither church was clearly dominant, religion could often become a particularly divisive issue even between men of similar social standing. In one deposition, that of Knogher Mac Gilpatrick O'Mullan, a quarrel was recorded between Art Mac Tomlin O'Mullan and Brian Mac Shane O'Mullan over religion, the substance of which was later admitted to by both parties. Art accused Brian, 'thou art a church warden yet do not attend thy office according to instructions. You had sixteen masses said in your house by Gillecome Mac Tadhg, abbot, and then relieved the said Gillecome and harboured him in your house as well as abroad'. Both men were native Irish and of some substance, both leasing a considerable amount of land from the Haberdashers' company around Artikelly but yet religion had emerged as a powerful divisive issue between them.[74]

Some of the strength of this type of division can be seen in the role of the friar who played such an important part in the depositions of those involved in Brian Crossagh's part of the plot. He is called Father O'Mullarkey but, as we have seen, it was unlikely to have been Edmond O'Mullarkey who was in Rome at the time, but probably another Franciscan priest. Such men were beginning to return to Ireland from the newly established continental seminaries, especially Louvain, where they were being trained. The Franciscans, drawn mainly from the Gaelic Irish community, were by far the most numerous and most politically active order in early seventeenth century Ireland. In 1623 of about 1,100 clergy in Ireland about 200 were Franciscans, 100 from other religious orders and 800 were secular or diocesan clergy.[75] Their continental experience had made them particularly sensitive to what they regarded as the evil doings of the 'heretic' in Ireland. Thus national identity and religious belief frequently became intertwined, as we shall see below. Thus the comments of the friar to Dermot O'Dunn that those who died with

V G O
CONTE DI TIRONE
GENERALE IBERNESE.

ON era sì forte la catena, con cui la
facrilega Iezabella d'Inghilterra, volea
ftrangolare le cofcienze de' Cattolici
nella Ibernia, che frà effi per fauore del
Cielo non fi truouaffe qualche Sanfone,
cui deffe il cuore di ftrapparla, per for-
marne ferri d'ignominia al nome di quella Sacrilega, che
auendo vn Capo pien d'errori volle farfi adorare come Capo della Chiefa Anglicana. Per fare,che l'Inghilterra com-
pariffe vn Moftro d'empietà, fol baftaua quel Capo, che di
capo altro non auea che l'effere più alto, per effere più da
vicino

Reputed likeness of Sir Hugh O'Neill, second earl of Tyrone, from Primo Damaschino, La Spada d'Orione Stellata nel Cielo di Marte. *Rome, 1680.*

O'Doherty had gone straight to heaven would not have been exceptional and may have played a role in encouraging some to conspire.

There were other binding forces which held the conspiracy together. The most obvious of these was the complex network of kinship which centred on the marriages of the earls of Tyrone and bound many of the plotters together. Alexander's grandfather, for example, was married to Mary O'Neill, daughter of the first earl of Tyrone. His uncle, Randal, was married to Alice daughter of Hugh, the second earl, who was Brian Crossagh's uncle. One of Alice's sisters, Rose, had been married to Sir Donnell O'Cahan, the father of Rory. The connections did not end there since there were also marriage connections between the O'Donnells and O'Neills. Niall Garbh's grand uncle had been married to the same Rose, daughter of Tyrone, who was later to marry Sir Donnell. Thus a complex series of intermarriages linked the plotters.[76]

In addition to these bonds of natural kinship there were also several layers of artificially created social bonds. Many of the plotters had been bound together by the structures of Gaelic Ulster which were not destroyed with the settlement of the province after 1607. The structures had, rather, been modified. Many native Irish contemporaries continued to describe their experience in terms of the language of Gaelic Ireland. In Dermot O'Dunn's first deposition, for example, Sir Toby Caulfield is not described as Con O'Neill's guardian but as his 'fosterer', as native Irish lords of the sixteenth century would have described him. Again in Cormac Mac Redmond Moyle Maguire's deposition he referred to Donough Mac Sweeney by his traditional title of 'chief of his name' as would have been customary in the sixteenth century. Other native Irish social customs also survived. The practice of 'commyns' still survived to bind lord and follower as we have seen above. Other similar native obligations bound many of the conspirators together. The custom of 'buyings', the giving of gifts to curry favour which was widely commented on by observers of native Irish society, was used on at least one occasion when Dermot O' Dunn approached Brian Crossagh with the entreaty 'if thou wilt give me a buying to be thy friend I will give thee a buying to be my friend'. Fosterage was another important social bonding practice in Gaelic Ireland and also played a place in drawing the conspirators together. According to Tadhg O'Lennan's second deposition Brian O'Laverty became involved in the conspiracy because he was foster father to Alexander Macdonnell.

While these old bonds were retained, new ones were also formed in the rapidly changing society of early seventeenth century Ulster. One such bond, that of retainer and follower is of some interest for the conspiracy. A number of those who were said to be involved were part of Macdonnell's household and they were virtually under the protection of their lord. This is most clearly illustrated in the case of Tadhg O'Lennan who, when he was first arrested, denied before Sir Thomas Phillips that he knew anything of the conspiracy and because 'he had Alexander Macdonnell's pass in regard thereof they gave credit to his words'. In a society where land was plentiful and population low tenants and servants were an invaluable asset and had to be treated with great care. Many lords went to great lengths to do so and the pass was effectively a warning that anyone dealing with O'Lennan would also have to deal with his master.[77]

In the new order of the seventeenth century such contacts were important as powerful men were essential to help their followers in times of difficulty. Pardons for offences were notoriously easy to obtain from the Dublin government, a fact commented on by many Dublin administrators. They were supposed to be granted by the Privy Council as a whole but in practice were usually granted by the lord deputy himself with the signatures of the rest of the Council being added later.[78] However one had to have a contact in the Dublin administration to avail of this service and it was usually a landlord who provided the contact. Shane Mac David, who had fled with Tyrone in 1607, for example used Captain Vaughan, a Donegal landlord, as an intermediary to bribe Chichester with £30 to obtain a licence for his wife to leave Ireland in 1615.[79] The desperation of men who had no such contact was well demonstrated in 1623 when a number of O'Neills in Armagh took Sir Benjamin Thorneborough prisoner and demanded that he write to the lord deputy for a pardon for them for some unspecified offences of which they had been accused they not having any contacts themselves. They were ultimately unsuccessful and had to surrender.[80] Clearly links with men of influence were not only desirable but essential in an age in which the central administration was exercising increasing control in the localities and it is hardly surprising that followers became involved in a plot in which their masters were among the chief movers.

Powerful though these bonds were they should not be overstressed. They did not provide the rationale for the plot, but simply shaped a common ground for the conspirators and provided a way in which new men could be recruited as the plan developed. At heart the conspirators were individualists, the bonds explaining more the sort of genealogical and social forces which selected the people for that particular conspiracy rather than the actual decision to conspire.

4. The Trial

The conspirators appear to have been more a collection of aggrieved men with very diverse types of grievances, bound together by social and religious forces, than instigators of a carefully laid plot masterminded by the exiled earl of Tyrone to stage a return and overthrow the new order. It is relatively easy to see this with the advantage of hindsight and the ability to piece together disparate fragments of evidence which were not readily available to contemporaries. But it was certainly not obvious to the assize judges for county Londonderry who were to try the case at the end of July 1615. Fears of invasion and rebellion had not subsided since the plot was first uncovered. The earl of Tyrone was still believed to be on his way back to Ireland and contemporaries saw many real or imaginary portends of his coming. In June, for example, the lord deputy noted that he thought that the number of Jesuits and friars had increased suddenly, and believed that the native Irish were expecting Tyrone that summer.[81]

Despite these circumstances the trial was, in many ways, unremarkable. Two assize judges, together with the mayor of Derry who sat in the court *ex officio*, were appointed to try the case. Both the assize judges, Sir John Davies, the attorney general who had regularly ridden the Ulster circuit previously, and Dominic Sarsfield, the chief justice of Common Pleas, knew something of the background of the case. Sarsfield had been present when Gorie Mac Manus O'Cahan's deposition had been taken in Dublin and Davies, as speaker of the House of Commons and a member of the Privy Council would have been well aware of Chichester's views on the plot. Davies' background as a lawyer, political theorist and administrator is well known but Sarsfield's story is more shadowy.[82] Born the son of an Old English merchant family in Cork he entered the Middle Temple in London, a favourite haunt for Irishmen training in the law, in 1594. The family's religious background is not known but it is likely that it was Catholic. Dominic, however, conformed to protestantism although whether it was an outward conformity or a real conversion is unclear since his son later became a Catholic, apparently with his father's blessing. Certainly his conformity did Dominic no harm in the promotion stakes. When he returned to Ireland he held a series of provincial legal posts in Munster, including that of chief justice of Munster. He then rose through the various levels of justice of the king's bench and second justice of the king's bench before being appointed chief justice of common pleas in November 1610 as a result of Sir John Davies's patronage. His appointment was renewed in 1616 but not without some difficulties with his patent. He acquired a substantial estate in Munster, was created a baronet in 1619, Viscount Kinsale in 1625, and Viscount Killmallock in 1627. His downfall came in the early 1630s when he was accused of attempting to lean on a jury in a politically very sensitive case involving allegations of malpractice on the part of the lord deputy. He was tried in the court of Star Chamber in England, fined and removed from the bench. He died in 1636 and was buried in Christ's Church, Cork.[83]

Another element in the trial of the conspirators was the jury appointed to evaluate the evidence and pronounce the verdict. The jury members were supposed to be representative of the county as a whole, being drawn from the freeholders of the county. The selection of representative jurors was not an easy exercise. Many Ulster landlords were unwilling to create freeholds because of the legal rights which they conferred on the tenant. Freeholds were held in perpetuity and so rents could not be increased as they were when leases expired – a considerable disadvantage in an age when speculative profit was the aim of most settler landlords. Landlords had fewer rights over freeholders than over leaseholders, they could not, for example, distrain a freeholder for unpaid rents. It is hardly surprising that landlords were unwilling to create freeholds. According to Nicholas Pynnar, who surveyed the plantation scheme in 1619, out of 1,974 British families in the settlement of the plantation counties only 334 were freeholders and in the case of Londonderry of 119 British families only 25 were freeholders.[84] Not only were freeholders uncommon, they were also not particularly wealthy. As the Commissioners who surveyed the plantation in 1622 noted 'some of those that are made [freeholders] have so small quantities of land and pay such dear rents or steep fines as they are not able to attend at the assize and quarter sessions and some make their own children freeholders'.[85] The same point was made by the freeholders of Loughinsholin barony, in county Londonderry, who complained of the expense involved in travelling to the assize in Derry twice a year, sometimes up to 30 or 40 shillings out of an annual income of £4 or £5.[86] Of the fifteen man jury which was to try the conspirators eleven came from the two main towns of Coleraine and Derry.

The pool of suitable jurors was yet further reduced by the unwillingness of the central government to allow native Irish freeholders to serve on grand juries. It was felt that they would refuse to return indictments against other native Irishmen, especially over the issue of recusancy. In many areas there was, however, little choice since there were simply not enough willing settlers appearing at the court to form a jury. The fears that the native Irish jurors would not find offences against each other were certainly well founded to judge from the number of native Irish who appeared at the Dublin court of Castle Chamber for failure to present bills, especially against recusants.[87] Even if a sufficient pool of men were available to form a jury there was no guarantee that they would all turn up on the right day and at the right place, a shortcoming they shared with contemporary English juries. Such organisation was the responsibility of the county sheriff and his sub-sheriffs who were responsible for preparing a list of the freeholders in the county from which the judges would nominate a jury.[88] Most of the members of the jury were to be settlers, although the accused could challenge individual jurors.

In addition to the problem with jurors the quality of these sheriffs and sub-sheriffs in the early seventeenth century was often poor but because of the limited pool of talent available there was little alternative to accepting what was available, efficient or otherwise.[89] A case in point is Richard Kirby who was sheriff of Londonderry for eight successive years from 1630 despite the fact that the central government was well aware that he was withholding money which should have been paid to the Exchequer and that he favoured Catholic clergy.[90] The problem did not stop with sheriffs. All branches of local administration were handicapped by a shortage of suitable personnel to serve in offices. It was difficult to find enough men to act as justices of the peace, who were the cornerstone of local government, and both of the parish constables who feature in the depositions were native Irish, one of whom was also a Catholic.[91]

For the trial of the conspirators a jury of fifteen men was empanneled to try the case.[92] It was normal practice to have two juries: a 'grand' jury who would find whether or not there was a case to answer and subsequently a 'petty' jury which would actually try the case. The gaol delivery roll makes mention of only one jury and it may be that given the difficulty in forming a jury the same group of men performed both functions. The jurors included two native Irish men, Sir Manus O'Cahan of Lisbebrarer, Rory's uncle, and Richard O'Cahan of Ballymacloskie. The settler element was in some ways unrepresentative of the county, being mainly urban in origin, but in other ways was not untypical of the settler community as a whole. Settlers had diverse origins and different motivations for participating in the Ulster plantation scheme and the jurors were no exception. Some, such as Henry Vaughan, were ex-army officers who had fought in Ireland during the Nine Year's War and had been encouraged to stay there because their pensions would not be paid in England and because cheap land was easily available as part of the plantation scheme. Soldiers were assigned a special role in the plantation and were given land on special terms because their military experience might be required to defend the settlement. Henry was granted 1,000 acres in the barony of Kilmacrennan, county Donegal but lived most of time in Derry where he was an alderman and where he served as mayor between 1625 and 1627.[93]

Other settlers on the jury had come to Ulster through trade contacts. These included Edmund Hayward who was a carrier and merchant in Coleraine and later bought land beside that of Nicholas Gill, in whose house the plot had first been hatched.[94] Yet others had more humble origins. Anthony Lipsitt was a carpenter who had come to work for the Londoners in the building of houses in Derry.[95] Yet others came as administrators or were relatives of administrators who were involved in setting up the plantation scheme. The most important of these was John Rowley, the agent of the London companies in Londonderry, and the man whom the conspirators intended to seize as hostage to be used in bargaining. Rowley himself was not on the jury but his brother, Nathaniel, who was burgess of Coleraine and later held land on the Drapers' estate and in Donegal, was.[96] Also on the jury was John Rowley's secretary, Paul Brasier, another burgess of Coleraine who also held lands from the bishop of Derry.[97] Whatever their origins the Londonderry settlement offered much more opportunity for advancement than these men would have had at home. Baptist Jones, for example, may have been an army officer in Carrickfergus and, after an unsuccessful attempt to become a servitor in the plantation scheme, he formed a partnership with John Rowley in 1617 to lease the Vintners' proportion for £120 a year. Like many of the new settlers Jones had little cash to back up his schemes. He paid one year's rent and then borrowed £500 from his landlord on the security of his lease. When Jones died in 1624 he had repaid neither capital nor interest and could have been up to £500 in arrears with his rent.[98]

Almost nothing is known of the attitude of these settler jurors to the native Irish or to the highland Scots. However any animosity which was borne against them was mitigated by economic necessity. The settler population of Londonderry was small by reference to the amount of land which had to be settled and although it had been part of the original agreement that the native Irish would be removed from the land by May 1615 this had not happened because of the shortage of suitable settler tenants to replace them. On the Vintners' proportion managed by Baptist Jones, who, by his lease, was specifically forbidden to take Irish as tenants, 184 out of 264 tenants in 1622 were native Irish. Furthermore, Jones had been part of a delegation which had gone to the lord deputy in 1617 to argue that some native Irish should be kept on the Londoners' lands.[99] The depositions taken after the discovery of the conspiracy also contain indications that if the settlers and natives were not firm friends they were certainly managing to co-exist with each other in mutual toleration.

Many of the native Irish were already, within six years of the plantation scheme being initiated, bilingual, being able to speak both Irish and English. It seems also that many of the settlers could speak Irish, an example being John Cornewall and Thomas Walle, the two English servants of Sir Toby Caulfield who were interpreters at an examination at Charlemount. There was also some intermarriage between settlers and natives from the earliest stages of the settlement. Brian Crossagh O'Neill's sister, for example, was married to the settler William Stewart, whom Brian hoped might become part of the plot. Other traces of settler influence can also be detected in matters such as dress. Most of the native Irish referred to in the depositions are described as wearing mantles, long blanket-like garments which enveloped the whole body, although the upper classes wore more English style clothes. The mantle was widely regarded by English commentators as a sign of native Irish barbarism since it marked them off from the more 'civil' English. There had been a number of attempts to forbid the wearing of them, including a proclamation of 1624 which ordered that anyone found wearing Irish dress was to be stripped and the garments cut up before him.[100] Some of the native Irish recorded in the depositions were already beginning to wear items of English style clothing, Brian O'Mullan being seen on the green at Limavady wearing his mantle and an English style hat. Such hats, along with other English style clothes, such as stockings, were being imported into Derry and Coleraine in large quantities in the early years of the settlement. Over 500 men's hats, for example, were imported into Coleraine in 1613, which was more than sufficient for the settler community, and in one ship alone, the *Seaflower* of Dover, a Coleraine merchant, Paul Brasier, imported over 300 pairs of stockings in May 1614. More luxurious items were also being brought in such as tobacco, silk ribbons, fine linens, various dyes and household items such as pewter plates, knives, forks and spoons.[101] It would seem likely that these also made their way into the hands of many native Irish who must have begun to appear more English in their speech, dress and manners than before.

The trial of the conspirators followed the normal course of an early seventeenth century trial as far as can be judged from the gaol delivery roll which was the formal record of the proceedings.[102] The indictment, which followed closely the sequence of events which can be reconstructed from the depositions with some small additions (such as the naming of the bishop of Derry as a hostage to be taken, taken from the depositions now lost) was read, and the conspirators entered a plea of not guilty from the bar of the court. The jury was chosen, and the prisoners had some right of challenge. The jury was then sworn and the king's counsel presented the case using sworn witnesses and the depositions. The conspirators could call unsworn witnesses but it is not known whether or not they did so. The judge summed up and then the jury consulted to find their verdict. All of this procedure was probably not unfamilar to the plotters. Just as the native Irish were absorbing language, dress and manners from the settlers so too they readily used English law to settle their disputes. Certainly from 1603 an increasing number of Ulster Irish resorted to the Dublin courts, especially the court of Chancery, to resolve disputes over land and debts. Native Irish also appeared frequently at the more local courts such as the assize and the manorial courts.[103] By the 1630s a knowledge of English law among the native community was not only useful but socially acceptable. The county Antrim poet Fear Flatha Ó Gnímh, for instance, listed a detailed knowledge of the English common law as one of the social graces of his patron, Sir Henry O'Neill.[104]

The verdict of the jurors on the trial evidence was a mixed one. There was not, as might perhaps have been expected of seventeenth century juries, a mass conviction as a deterrent to others, secured by suitable pressure by the judges or other royal officials. Six were found guilty: Rory O'Cahan, Brian Crossagh O'Neill, Loughlin O'Laverty, Gorie Mac Manus O'Cahan, Cuconnacht O'Keenan and Arthur Mac Donnell O'Neill. The punishment was a mandatory one: to be drawn through the streets of Derry in chains to the gallows where they would be hanged but when only half dead to be cut down, disembowelled, beheaded, the body quartered and then burnt. It was also normal to display the heads of the executed men above the gates of the city as a warning to anyone who might wish to emulate their treason. The other eleven accused, including Alexander Macdonnell, were acquitted.

The verdict having been arrived at there was little to do but tidy up the administrative loose ends. The innocent were released to make their own way in the world. Chichester was reluctant to release the most prominent, and in his own way the most ruthless, Alexander Macdonnell, who was clearly the originator of the plot. He demanded good sureties for Alexander's behaviour, which was not in the least surprising given that his brother, Sorley, was then involved in an uprising in Scotland with some of the conspirators who had escaped. As a result Alexander was still in prison in September 1615 but was released shortly afterwards. He lived another nineteen years and the social ambitions which prompted him to plot were eventually fulfilled. He was created a baronet in 1627 and built up a substantial estate in county Antrim. By the 1650s when the Cromwellians confiscated the estate from his son it amounted to over seven and a half thousand acres in the barony of Kilconway.[105]

The guilty were, of course, punished. Brian Crossagh O'Neill was executed almost immediately and his estate forfeited to the crown. In June 1616 his lands were granted to Francis Edgeworth.[106] His younger brother Con, who was not involved in the plot fled to the continent, arriving in Brussels probably in February 1616. Albert, Archduke of Austria and Governor of the Spanish Netherlands, wrote to Philip III of Spain that Con had arrived there 'on account of the English having tried to make him a prisoner, as I have heard, and because some months ago they had beheaded his brother on the charge that he had tried to rise out in rebellion'. He asked the king for help with his maintenance and studies and then to 'serve your Majesty after the example of his ancestors'. Following the intervention of the earl of Tyrone he was granted a pension of fifty crowns monthly as part of the establishment of the Irish regiment in the Netherlands and a further grant of six crowns was made in July 1621. He became a soldier in the regiment of Captain Charles O'Neill who, like Con, was a nephew of the earl of Tyrone. At this juncture Con disappears from the historian's view.[107]

The execution of the others was delayed. This situation was a source of some concern to Chichester. He wrote to the King in September 1615:

> that we know them [the remaining five found guilty] to be men apt to rise with every storm that shall threaten us and of the brood of rebels who will never be loyal nor conform themselves to any laudable or civil course of life we have directed the judges to give order for their execution which they have done. And rather for fear that they should break prison and so escape to Sir James Macdonnell and other Scottish rebels unto whom they were neighbours and some of them were of kindred and alliance.[108]

The eventual fate of those in prison is clear. Rory O'Cahan was certainly hanged since his freehold was resumed by the London Companies and let to George Carey, recorder of the city of Derry for his life at £5 6s. 8d. a year.[109] Above the names of three others on the gaol delivery roll, Gorie Mac Manus O'Cahan. Cuconnacht O'Keenan and Loughlin O'Laverty, is noted 'ss': suspensus – hanged! There were also the inevitable minor problems to be resolved. Some of those who had been involved in the plot had not been brought to trial either because there was insufficient evidence available to secure a conviction or because their part was not large enough to warrant the trouble of a trial. They were, however, no longer considered trustworthy. Two native Irishmen involved in the plot who held freeholds from the crown, Owen Mac Cawell and Turlough Moyle Maguire, had their lands resumed and granted to settlers.[110]

5. From Traitors to Saints

Following trial and sentence the rather sordid events of the conspiracy passed rapidly from the public mind. Several developments made this possible. The ending of the parliamentary session in May 1615 and its subsequent dissolution in October took some heat out of the political scene. The death of the earl of Tyrone on the continent in 1616 also eased the situation since it removed the immediate threat of an invasion from the continent. Finally the recall of Chichester as lord deputy and his promotion to lord treasurer in England in November 1615 led to the appointment of Oliver St John, who was one of those who had not really believed in the reality of the conspiracy, as lord deputy in July 1616. The conspiracy was all but forgotten in Ireland. Even the memory of the centrepiece of the conspiracy, Con O'Neill, faded, and the writer of the *Aphorismical Discovery of Treasonable Faction* written shortly after 1652 referred to the sons of the earl of Tyrone as Brian and Sean – Con being entirely forgotten.[111] No one was to mention the plot for almost a century except its discoverer, Sir Thomas Phillips. Phillips was not beyond pointing out to Charles I in 1629 when attacking the London Companies, who he considered had defrauded him of land and made a poor job of developing the Londonderry plantation, that it was he who had saved the settlement:

> But your Majesty's greatest loss consists in the filling of the country with Irish at whose mercy the few English lie for they may at their pleasure surprise their houses, cut their throats and possess their arms, and had done so had I not happily discovered a combination of the ablest and most dangerous gentlemen of the North to have burnt and destroyed their whole plantation towns and country and thereupon the 9th of April 1615 they were apprehended and I sent them to the lord deputy when his lordship after examination sent to receive their trial at the Derry assizes where six of them were executed being Tyrone's near kinsmen. The same plot was then likewise discovered by Mr Trumball, his Majesty's agent in Brussels has certified into England.[112]

Phillips, however was well known for seeing many plots – real and imaginary, mostly the latter – and on this occasion was clearly interested in upgrading the conspiracy to a major rebellion to impress the king. Trumball's reports, for example, were no more than comments that Tyrone was on the move rather than that he was conspiring.[113] But since the whole plot was assumed by Phillips to be a masterplan by the earl of Tyrone to bring down the plantation, the detail of the wording seemed irrelevant to him.

If discussion of the plot and the events surrounding it virtually ceased among the administration in Ireland it was only beginning elsewhere. From the end of the sixteenth century a considerable Irish community had been growing in continental Europe. It had begun with the establishment of colleges at Douai in 1594 and Antwerp in 1600 mainly to train the younger sons of the Old English of the Pale for the priesthood. In the early seventeenth century this movement quickened with the founding of further colleges as more people left Ireland after the Nine Year's War and the flight of the earls. The most influential of these foundations was the Franciscan college of St Anthony at Louvain founded in 1607. Louvain was to become the centre of the Gaelic Irish on the continent. Almost exclusively Ulster in its composition, it became a meeting place for exiles, such as Owen Roe O'Neill, who had joined the Spanish forces in the Netherlands.[114] There these sort of men met with the stark doctrines of the Counter-Reformation, especially the idea that Ireland was being run by heretics.

There also ideas of nationality became simplified by two developments, a detachment from the complexities of Irish politics and society and the need to defend themselves against the equally nationalist Scots on the continent who wished to claim the early saints of Ireland for themselves. It was this sort of environment which could produce large scale national works such as the *Annals of the Four Masters*, the *Lives of the Saints of Ireland* and the *Genealogies of the Saints and Kings*. Even when these clerics returned to Ireland they were capable of producing the grand work such as Geoffrey Keating's *Foras Feasa ar Eirinn*. These were the men who were convinced that the old order was dying and had to be preserved with such work, sentiments which do not appear to have been shared by many of those within Ireland who were little exposed to the new ideas being developed on continental Europe. Indeed one of these continentally trained clerics, Father Robert Chamberlain, who attempted to intervene in a traditional poetic dispute between the poets of the North and the South, crying 'Woe to him who awakens their strife' was told 'it would be better for you to attend to your office'.[115]

Given this attitude towards Ireland, which developed among the exiles during the early seventeenth century, it was not surprising that they took an interest in the conspiracy and interpreted it as a clash on nationalist and religious lines between the persecuted Catholic Irish and the heretic settler. As early as late July 1615 a Franciscan friar from Louvain, Hugh Mac Caghwell, told the papal representative at Brussels of the arrest and trial of 'noblemen, kinsmen of the Count of Tyrone' and he in turn informed the cardinal secretary of state in Rome: a move of some importance given the state of relations between the papacy and Tyrone.[116] The Jesuits in their Annual Letter for 1615 gave a more detailed account of events. They recounted the almost accidental arrest of O'Lennan 'who used to devote his days to gambling, sporting and drinking bouts'. Their version recorded that O'Lennan, in fear of being hanged under the martial law which the provost marshal exercised, invented a story about the conspiracy. Several noblemen were consequently seized, thrown into chains and interrogated on the rack and finally hanged. This, according to the letter, created great fear among the Ulster Catholics who feared that any 'contemptible idler' might raise similar charges against them.[117]

The matter was raised in a continental context again a year later in June 1616 when Sorley Macdonnell arrived at Dunkirk with fifty-two followers, rather more than the twenty-four or twenty-five who had left Ireland with him in a small fishing boat in May 1615, after a certain amount of piracy and involvement in trouble in the Scottish Isles. They were taken prisoner, four were executed and twenty-four were condemned to the galleys. The remainder fled before they could be seized. Petitions, probably from native Irish on the continent, to the Spanish King Philip persuaded him to remit the sentences. These men were, according to the petitions, 'some very close relatives of the highest nobility of the Highlands and Islands of both kingdoms [Ireland and Scotland] who to escape from the persecution of the heretics who sought to behead them (on the false charge that they sought to rise in rebellion with certain strongholds and forts on that coast)' had come there.[118] Already the story of the conspiracy was growing: this version suggested that high nobility was involved rather than penniless younger sons, and upwards of a fifty were reportedly going to be executed rather than the six who actually were.

The two most important continentally influenced commentators on the events of 1615 were David Rothe the Catholic bishop of Ossory, and the first bishop to be appointed in seventeenth century Ireland, and Philip O'Sullivan Beare, a Munster exile in Spain. Rothe, the son of an Old English merchant family in Kilkenny, had been educated for the priesthood at the continental colleges of Douai and Salamanca. His most influential work, the *Analecta Sacra* was published at Cologne sometime between 1616 an 1619. It was addressed to Charles, then prince of Wales but later to succeed his father as king of England in

1625. The body of the work was a collection of the sufferings of Catholics under Elizabeth and James. To Rothe the conspiracy was entirely fictitious, dreamt up by an infamous gambler (O'Lennan) who was in danger of being executed before it was suggested to him by an official that he might save himself by inventing a conspiracy. Thus, Rothe argued, the nobility were betrayed by 'a pitiful, uneducated, barbarous rustic' who was used by the government to deprive the Irish Catholics of their good name and 'provoke the traditional inhabitants . . . [and] . . . to send them all away from their own seats and their ancient heritage'. The marginal notes drew a parallel between the 'nobles subjected to the rack and hanged' and the experiences of the early Christians under Nero and Justinian.[119]

Philip O'Sullivan Beare took a not dissimilar line in his *Historiae Catholicae Hiberniae Compendium* published at Lisbon in 1621 with the sanction of the Holy Inquisition and Philip of Spain. Philip O'Sullivan Beare was the younger son of Dermot O'Sullivan who had been involved both in the rebellion of James Fitzmaurice Fitzgerald in 1569 and with O'Neill during the Nine Year's War. He had gone to Spain in 1602 as a boy and remained there strongly influenced by Counter-Reformation catholicism. His motive in writing the *Historiae* was set out in the introduction 'To the Catholic Reader'. He was to chronicle the deeds of the invincible martyrs, pious confessors, and soldiers who had fought against the heretic English. His version of the events of 1615 conforms to this set of pre-suppositions. It was Chichester, in O'Sullivan's version of events, who, greedy for land, ordered the arrest of 'a man of depraved character and addicted to gambling' who was then promised immunity and reward if he accused some 'Ulstermen who were seen to be outstanding in bravery and intellect'. O'Sullivan held that there was no evidence against the six 'knights of high lineage', who did not confess to anything but were tried before 'twelve Scots and English heretics who wished for the death of the defendants all the more because they had lands in Ulster and detested the proximity of Catholics'. According to this account all six, including Alexander Macdonnell, were hanged, drawn and quartered as were two others, O'Keenan, the letter writer, who was here elevated to the status of a priest, and O'Murray who like the others was given a knighthood by O'Sullivan.[120]

The factual difficulties in both accounts are clear but the exaggerations in O'Sullivan's account are especially graphic. The social standing of the conspirators was inflated, the conspiracy was given a unity which never existed, the fact that many conspirators were Scots was forgotten, the make-up of the jury was misconstrued and both the sufferings and the numbers executed were exaggerated. Also the lowly social status of O'Lennan was highlighted. He was portrayed as an underling used to destroy the nobility. We know little about O'Lennan's actual status. From the depositions it appears he was a servant of Alexander Macdonnell's and one deponent, Absie Lowe, went as far as to suggest that he may have been a tenant of Alexander's. Certainly he had some education as he was literate in both Irish and English. At the time of the conspiracy he was certainly in debt. However it was not O'Lennan who actually exposed the conspiracy. Dermot og O'Dunn had already exposed the conspiracy before O'Lennan was arrested for the first time and O'Dunn's first deposition was taken six days before O'Lennan's.

The effect of these changes in the story was twofold. First it made the story more acceptable to the native Irish themselves. Gaelic Ireland was an essentially aristocratic society in which the doings of the lower orders were of little concern to anyone unless they impinged on the rights of their lord. As Geoffrey Keating made clear in the preface to his *Foras Feasa ar Eireann*, his was to be a proper history, the history of the nobility, in contrast to the writings of those who had attacked Ireland, such as Edmund Spenser and Richard Stanihurst, who took 'notice of the ways of inferiors and wretched little hags, ignoring the worthy actions of the gentry'.[121] Thus for the story of the conspiracy to be relevant to the Irish both at home and in Europe it had to be concerned with the deeds of the gentry. Secondly, from a more Counter-Reformation perspective the changes were required to make the conspiracy appear as another example of the genocidal policy towards the true Catholic nobility of Ireland being pursued by the heretic using underhand means. The same point was made by both Rothe and O'Sullivan and was common to many Irish writers on the continent during the early seventeenth century who had a view of events which was denied to those at home. As the Dominican, Dominic O'Daly, who spent much time in Portugal, wrote in his *History of the Geraldines*, 'the whole of the Irish nobility may now be described as totally extinct' and 'even as I write ruin is hovering over the land'.[122]

There was some attempt by the Dublin government to reply to this position. In 1624 Thomas Ryves, one of the judges in the Irish ecclesiastical court, replied to Rothe's *Analecta* in his *Regiminis Anglicani in Hibernia defensio adversus Analecten*. Rothe's was probably the most important view to attack since it was circulating widely in Ireland and at least one translation from Latin into English had been made of part of it in the early seventeenth century.[123] Ryves viewed Rothe's allegations over the treatment of the conspirators as the most serious of the charges levied against the government. He offered a rather different version of events to that set out by Rothe, arguing on secular grounds that the plot was a serious threat to the country.

Following O'Lennan's confession, he pointed out that others, including O'Cahan had also confessed (although O'Cahan's confession which is also known from other sources to have existed is now lost) and that the depositions taken from various sources, tended to corroborate each other. He justified the use of torture on purely judicial grounds. O'Lennan's social standing was a non-issue for Ryves 'for who would be so simple that if he heard a dog barking in the night would not act on this evidence for his own safety' and he proceeded to cite a number of classical precedents for this action.[124]

At this point the debate quietly subsided. There were to be few scares of rebellion in Ulster before 1641 to regenerate the debate. A notable exception was the year 1625 when rumours of war with Spain roused old fears among the Dublin administration about a rising in Ireland on the principle that England's difficulty was Ireland's opportunity. Sir William Cole, the settler landlord of Enniskillen, managed to confirm those fears by uncovering a plot among a number of Maguires in Fermanagh.[125] In general, however, the fears of the settlers in Ulster which had been so marked at the beginning of the century subsided as time went on. They took less care to protect themselves than they had done before. In 1630, for example, a muster of the armed men among the settlers revealed that they were even more poorly armed than they had been in 1619. In 1630 about 13,000 men in the six planted counties could muster only about one musket between thirty-three men whereas in 1619 one man in eight had a musket. Other arms were also in shorter supply than they had been eleven years earlier.[126] Settlers were also beginning to abandon the fortified castles with bawnes which they had built in the early years of the settlement in favour of much less heavily fortified manor houses like those of Jacobean England. Sir Toby Caulfield, for instance, who had lived with Con O'Neill in Charlemount fort at the beginning of the century, chose to build his new house at Castle Caulfield almost without any built-in defensive features at all.[127]

The 1630s were to bring more heated issues to a head with the lord deputyship of Thomas Wentworth, earl of Strafford, who added new dimensions to the problem of governing Ireland. The clear cut divide of loyalty to the crown on the grounds of religion which had been the essence of Ryves's and Rothe's arguments was made more complex by new tensions which created different types of alienation from the Dublin government. These tensions gave rise to new frustrations which were to boil over in the rising of the native Irish in 1641. The rebellion seemed all the more wicked because it was so totally unexpected.[128]

To some later historians the profound differences between the reasons for the events of 1615 and those for the events of 1641 were not clear. What happened in 1615 was interpreted as a curtain raiser to the inevitability of a rebellion of a fundamentally disloyal people. As one of the most prominent southern Unionist historians of the late nineteenth century, Richard Bagwell, noted of the conspiracy 'the whole affair is important mainly as showing that the Ulster Irish were anxious to do then what they actually did do in 1641'.[129] Bagwell's comments were well accepted among certain groups in Ireland.

It was difficult for the nationalist camp to reply to this view since they admitted that the rising lacked some of the glory which should have been associated with the resurgence of native Ireland. E.A. D'Alton went as far as to describe the whole event as 'a stupid rebellion' in his *History of Ireland*, first published in 1912.[130] This work, which epitomised the faith and fatherland approach to the history of Anglo-Irish relations, was the standard bedside reading of the early twentieth century Irish nationalist. However a nationalist champion of the conspirators was to arise in the person of Tim Healy, lawyer and member of Parnell's Irish Party in the House of Commons. He had been expelled from the Irish Party in 1902 but survived long enough in political life to become the first Governor General of the newly established Free State in 1922.[131]

Healy's first venture into seventeenth century Ireland came in 1907 when he appeared as counsel for the defence in an action to determine the ownership of the Lough Neagh fishings. The case went to the House of Lords in 1911 with judgement being given against Healy who had represented the fishermen of the lough in their claim for public ownership of the fishings. The core of Healy's case was that Chichester, to whom the lough had been granted in the early seventeenth century, had obtained his grant by deceit and that it was therefore invalid. Not deterred by defeat Healy published his case as *Stolen Waters: a page in the conquest of Ulster* in 1913 and it was reissued in an abbreviated form in *The Great fraud of Ulster* in 1917.

For many years thereafter Healy produced a series of works which attacked Chichester's probity. It was not purely an intellectual exercise for as he put it 'The Imperial act of 1920 for the partition of the island [Ireland] is the complement and consequence of the policy of the Robber Deputy of 1605-15'. The last of these works, *The Victims of 1615*, published in 1921, contained his account of the conspiracy. It was intended to place the blame on Chichester's corrupt mis-government, and in particular his greed and dishonesty, for the torture and execution of 'the last survivors of Ulster's chivalry'. It illicited considerable public support in an age when Catholic nationalism was at its height. It even prompted a letter to Healy from a Dominican priest, Father M.H. MacInerney, headed 'Cause of the Irish Martyrs'.[132] This was no mere whim since Father MacInerney was no less a personage

Tim Healy, author of The Victims of 1615.

than the Vice Postulator of the Cause of the Irish Martyrs, the man who 'under God, [was] the prime mover in the whole undertaking' of making saints and martyrs.

The cause of the Irish martyrs had been growing in momentum since the publication in 1868 of Myles O'Reilly's *Memorials of those who suffered for the Catholic faith in Ireland in the 16th, 17th and 18th centuries*. The conspirators featured in this work, the evidence being drawn from the writings of O'Sullivan Beare complete with all the inaccuracies in that account of events.[133] In the early years of the twentieth century the cause of the Irish martyrs was being taken very seriously indeed following the example of the English Church which was vigorously pursuing the cause of its potential martyrs. In the process the English had engaged in a certain amount of ecclesiastical imperialism, laying claim to at least one whom the Irish regarded as one of their saints: Oliver Plunket, the former archbishop of Armagh, hanged at Tyburn during the Popish Plot of 1681. To prevent such naked piracy, and to demonstrate that Catholic Ireland could not be outstripped by Protestant England in the race for sancity, the search for suitable Irish candidates for martyrdom began in earnest and the plotters of 1615 were not overlooked.

By 1903, the preparations had been made and the first official stage of the Catholic church procedure towards beatification or canonisation was initiated. William J. Walsh, archbishop of Dublin and the man to whom *The Victims of 1615* was dedicated, presided over the Diocesan court at Dublin, which was assessing the evidence on the cases of almost 300 potential martyrs, prior to its being sent to Rome. The case of the six who were put to death in Derry in 1615 was among those considered. They fulfilled the basic requirements of martyrdom, which included having died a violent death for the faith. That they had died for the faith was deduced from the fact that the six had been put to death at the hands of the Dublin, and therefore Protestant, administration. In such circumstances it was felt it could be safely assumed that the victims had died for the faith. The case was further copper fastened by the fact that one of those hanged, Loughlin O'Laverty, had been a priest.

The second stage of the long bureaucratic procedure of obtaining a Declaration of Martyrdom, the Apostolic Process, got under way in 1915, and the case of the same six was still on the books. Father M.H. MacInerney was in charge of assembling the available evidence and seeing the many cases through their various stages. By Christmas 1920 the documentation on the six conspirators, among others, was ready for final despatch to Rome, and Father Dunne, the archbishop's secretary, having been given special diplomatic immunity because of the secret nature of the documents he was transporting, 'was sped upon the errand'. However, the lengthy and cumbersome procedures involved in promoting and assessing each cause meant that the cases under active consideration were subsequently whittled down to a handful. The cause of the conspirators did not survive this drastic pruning, and the documentation which had been carefully prepared by Walsh, MacInerney, and many others was left to gather dust in the office of the Sacred Congregation of Rites in the Vatican, where it presumably remains to this day.[134]

Thus the experience of the seventeenth century became part of the mythology and ecclesiastical politics of the twentieth. Yet the transformation was so complete that we may wonder what those who indulged in a little overzealous talk over a few drinks in Nicholas Gill's house would have thought of being made candidates for matyrdom. Alexander Macdonnell and Rory O'Cahan, two discontented younger sons, Brian Crossagh O'Neill, the social undesirable, Sorley Macdonnell, the pirate, Hugh O'Mergee, the one-eared man, Dalton Duff, the dwarf, and Hugh Mac Shane O'Neill the highway robber would have been bemused at the idea of of being national heroes let alone being in the company of saints.

Notes

1. T.C.D., MS 672, ff 61-93^v; there are excellent summaries of the depositions in *Cal. S.P. Ire., 1615-25*. Two of the original depositions have survived in P.R.O., SP 63/223/14, i, ii. Much of the evidence on which this essay is based is drawn from the depositions. Where no other source is indicated in the notes it can be assumed that the argument is based on the deposition evidence.

2. P.R.O., SP 63/233/14; *Commons Journals, Ireland*, (1753) i pp 43-4; Victor Treadwell, 'The Irish House of Lords in the Irish parliament of 1613-15' in *English Historical Review* 80 (1965), pp 92-107.

3. P.R.O., SP 63/233/15.

4. P.R.O., SP 63/233/18.

5. P.R.O., SP 63/233/16.

6. T.W. Moody, 'The Irish parliament under Elizabeth and James I' in *Proceedings of the Royal Irish Academy* 45 sect. C (1939), pp 57-71; *Cal. S.P. Ire., 1615-25*, p. 24.

7. Historical Manuscripts Commission, *Report on the Hastings Mss* (4 vols, London, 1930-47) iv, p. 7.

8. British Library, Lansdowne Ms 159, ff 164, 191, 205, 223.

9. *Commons Journals, England* (1742), i, p. 461; for the Addled Parliament see T.L. Moir, *The Addled Parliament of 1614* (Oxford, 1958).

10. *Commons Journals, Ireland*, i, p. 50.

11. Moody, 'Irish parliament', pp 61-3.

12. *Cal. S.P. Ire., 1615-25*, pp 53-4; *Acts of the Privy Council, 1615-16*, p. 138.

13. The legal basis of torture is set out in James Heath, *Torture and English law: an administrative and legal history* (Connecticut, 1986) and R.D. Melville, 'The use and forms of judicial torture in England and Scotland' in *Scottish Historical Review* 2 (1904) pp 225-49. *Cal. S.P. Ire., 1625-32*, pp 73, 191, 238, 296; J.T. Gilbert (ed.), *History of the Irish confederation and the war in Ireland* (7 vols. Dublin, 1882-91) i, p. 296; for the absence of a rack in Ireland, P.R.O., SP 63/174/5.

14. Bodleian Library, Oxford, Carte Ms 30, ff 50-58^v; R.D. Edwards (ed.), 'Letter book of Sir Arthur Chichester 1612-14' in *Analecta Hibernica* 8 (1938), p. 74; *Cal. S.P. Ire., 1611-14*, p. 324.

15. Philip Robinson, *The plantation of Ulster* (Dublin, 1984), pp 93, 223.

16. Blennerhasset's tract is printed in J.T. Gilbert (ed.), *A contemporary history of affairs in Ireland* (3 vols, Dublin, 1879) i, p. 319; T.W. Moody, *The Londonderry plantation* (Belfast, 1939), pp 329-30.

17. Edwards, 'Chichester letter book', p. 74.

18. David Stevenson, *Alasdair MacColla and the Highland problem in the seventeenth century* (Edinburgh, 1980), pp 35-47.

19. Sir Ralph Winwood, *Letters and memorials of state in the reign of Queen Elizabeth and King James*, ed. E. Sawyer, (3 vols. London, 1725), iii, pp 501-4; P.R.O., SP 63/232/21, 22; British Library, Cotton Titus B x, ff 238-8ᵛ; *Cal. S.P. Ire., 1615-25*, pp 20-2.

20. O'Neill's movements are dealt with by Micheline Kerney Walsh, *'Destruction by peace' Hugh O'Neill after Kinsale* (Armagh, 1986), pp 117-26, 129-40.

21. *Cal. S.P. Ire., 1608-10*, pp 3, 4, 37; Brendan Jennings (ed.), 'Brussels Ms 3947: Donatus Moneyus, De provincia Hiberniae S.Francisci' in *Analecta Hibernica* 6 (1934), pp 108, 114, 119, 121.

22. P.R.O., SP 63/233/19, printed in *Cal. S.P. Ire., 1615-25*, p. 52.

23. P.R.O.N.I., T 656/11; R.C. Simington, *The Civil Survey* (10 vols, Dublin 1931-61) iii, p. 149. The lands passed to John Pocock in 1658 (P.R.O.N.I., T 656/14) but the townland is still called 'Gills'.

24. *Calendar of patent rolls, Ireland, James I*, pp 250, 283.

25. *Cal. S.P. Ire., 1608-10*, p. 540.

26. Kenneth Nicholls, *Gaelic and gaelicised Ireland in the middle ages* (Dublin, 1972), pp 8-10.

27. T.W. Moody, J.G. Simms (eds), *The bishopric of Derry and the Irish Society of London* (2 vols, Dublin 1968-83) i, p. 80; *Cal. S.P. Ire., 1615-25*, p. 412; on this point generally, Peter Clark, 'The alehouse and the alternative society' in Donald Pennington, Keith Thomas (eds), *Puritans and revolutionaries* (Oxford, 1978), pp 47-72.

28. George O'Brien (ed.), *Advertisements for Ireland* (Dublin, 1923), p. 55.

29. *Cal. S.P. Ire., 1611-14*, p. 250; *Cal. S.P. Ire., 1615-25*, p. 282; *Cal Carew, 1603-25*, p. 161.

30. British Library, Additional Ms 18735, sumarised in *Cal. S.P. Ire., 1615-25*, pp 221-6; George Hill, *An historical account of the plantation in Ulster* (Belfast, 1877), p. 82.

31. *Cal. S.P. Ire., 1611-14*, p. 482; L. Boynton, 'The Tudor provost marshal' in *English Historical Review* 77 (1962), pp 437-55.

32. H.M.C., *Hastings Mss* iv, p. 48.

33. Aidan Clarke, *The Old English in Ireland* (London, 1966), p. 294.

34. Moody, *Londonderry plantation*, p. 167; Leeds City Library, Temple Newsham Papers, TN/PO7/I/4 a.

35. T.W. Moody (ed.), 'The school bills of Conn O'Neill at Eton' in *Irish Historical Studies* 2 (1940-1), pp 189-204; *Cal. S.P. Ire., 1615-25* p. 39; *Acts of the Privy Council, 1615-16* pp 138-9, 240, 243, 252. Caulfield's career is given in the patent creating him Baron Charlemont, *Cal. S.P. Ire., 1615-25*, pp 307-9.

36. Bernadette Cunningham, 'Native culture and political change in Ireland, 1580-1640' in Ciaran Brady, Raymond Gillespie (eds), *Natives and newcomers: essays on the making of Irish colonial society* (Dublin, 1986), pp 156-9. For dissatisfaction *Cal. S.P. Ire., 1608-10*, pp 499-500, 530-1; *Cal Carew, 1603-24*, p. 142.

37. Tomás Ó Raghallaigh (ed.), *Duanta Eoghain Ruaidh Mhic an Bhaird* (Galway, 1930), pp 118-21, especially lines 77-84.

38. Hill, *Plantation*, pp 246-7. Tadhg's account is Paul Walsh (ed.), *The flight of the earls* (Maynooth, 1916).

39. For one case study, Bernadette Cunningham, Raymond Gillespie, 'The east Ulster bardic family of Ó Gnímh' in *Éigse* 20 (1984) pp 106-14; for Brian og Ó Cianáin, Royal Irish Academy, Ms 936, f 1.

40. Ó Raghallaigh, *Duanta Eoghain Ruaidh*, pp 258-67.

41. T.H. Mullin, J.E. Mullan, *The Ulster clans* (Belfast, 1966), pp 77-98.

42. For landholding generally, Mary O'Dowd, 'Gaelic economy and society' in Brady and Gillespie (eds), *Natives and Newcomers*, pp 123-29. For O'Cahan, Myles Dillon, 'Ceart Uí Néill' in *Studia Celtica* 1 (1966), pp 1-18.

43. Nicholas Canny, 'The flight of the earls, 1607' in *Irish Historical Studies* 17 (1970-1), pp 391-5.

44. Mullin, Mullan, *The Ulster clans*, pp 96-8, 114-6, Bodleian Library, Oxford, Carte Ms 61, ff 334.

45. Sean O Domhnaill 'Sir Niall Garbh O'Donnell and the rebellion of Sir Cahir O'Doherty' in *Irish Historical Studies* 3 (1942-3), pp 34-8; Cyril Falls, 'Neill Garve: English ally and victim' in *Irish Sword* 1 (1949-53), pp 2-7.

46. *Cal. S.P. Domestic, 1611-18*, p. 148.

47. Historical Manuscripts Commission, *Fourth Report*, appendix, p. 283; *Cal. S.P. Ire., 1615-25*, p. 345.

48. *Cal. S.P. Ire., 1608-10*, pp 60, 67.

49. *Cal. S.P. Ire., 1608-10*, pp 67, 412-3; P.R.O., SP 63/232/19.

50. P.R.O., SP 63/255/226.

51. Hill, *Plantation*, pp 231-7.

52. *Cal. S.P. Ire., 1600-1*, p. 290.

53. P.R.O., SP 63/259/19; the history of the freeholds is traced in Mullin, Mullan, *The Ulster clans*, pp 153-72.

54. *Cal. S.P. Ire., 1608-10*, pp 503, 504-5.

55. T.W. Moody, 'Sir Thomas Phillips of Limavady, servitor' in *Irish Historical Studies* 1 (1938-9), pp 251-272.

56. Hill, *Plantation*, p. 249; *Cal. Carew, 1603-25*, p. 238; *Cal. pat. rolls Ire., Jas. I*, p. 187.

57. Edinburgh University Library, Laing Ms II no. 5.

58. For some examples, Raymond Gillespie, *Colonial Ulster: the settlement of east Ulster 1600-41* (Cork, 1985), p. 201.

59. D.A. Chart (ed), *Londonderry and the London Companies* (Belfast, 1928), p. 36; *Cal. S.P. Ire., 1611-14*, p. 273; H.M.C., *Hastings Mss* iv, p. 179.

60. Raymond Gillespie, *Colonial Ulster*, pp 87-8; *Cal. S.P. Ire., 1615-25*, pp 491-2.

61. On Sorley, Paul Walsh, 'Captain Somhairle Mac Domhnaill and his books' in Paul Walsh, *Irish chiefs and leaders* (Dublin,1960), pp 110-40; Stevenson, *Alasdair Mac Colla*, p. 107.

62. Eoin MacNeill, Gerard Murphy (eds), *Duanaire Finn* (3 vols, Irish texts society, London 1908-1953).

63. J. Maidment (ed.), 'Letters and papers relating to Irish matters from the Balfour Mss' in *Abbotsfort Club Miscellany* (Edinburgh, 1837) pp 278-9; British Library, Sloane Ms 3287, f. 62; Chart, *Londonderry*, pp 61-2.

64. S.J. Watts, *From border to middle shire: Northumberland 1586-1625* (Leicester, 1975), pp 39-41, 249-50; J.F. Ferguson (ed), 'The Ulster roll of gaol

delivery' in *Ulster Journal of Archaeology* 1st series 1 (1853), pp 261-70, 2 (1854), pp 25-8.

65. For the development of markets see Raymond Gillespie, 'The origins and development of an Ulster urban network, 1609-41' in *Irish Historical Studies* 24 (1984-5), pp 15-29 and Raymond Gillespie, 'Lords and commons in seventeenth century Mayo' in Raymond Gillespie and Gerard Moran (eds), '*A various country': essays in Mayo history 1500-1900* (Westport, 1987), pp 44-7. For woodkern using markets *Cal. S.P. Ire., 1625-32*, p. 216. The selling of stolen cattle was a major problem in the early seventeenth century and was the subject of a number of proclamations, e.g. R.R. Steele, *Tudor and Stuart proclamations* (2 vols Oxford, 1910), 2, part i, nos. 249, 264.

66. Moody, *Londonderry plantation* p. 330; *Cal. S.P. Ire., 1615-25* p. 86; *Cal. S.P. Ire., 1611-14*, p. 146.

67. *Cal. pat. rolls Ire., Jas. I*, pp 183, 227, 267.

68. *Cal. S.P. Ire., 1608-10*, p. 15.

69. Seamus Ó Ceallaigh, *Gleanings from Ulster history* (Cork, 1951), p. 114; *Cal. S.P. Ire., 1611-14*, p. 4.

70. Historical Manuscripts Commission, *Report on the manuscripts of the earl of Egmont* (2 vols, London, 1905-9), 1, part i, p. 35.

71. The list is printed in Mullin, Mullan, *The Ulster clans*, pp 220-2.

72. Chart, *Londonderry*, pp 46-7.

73. Alan Ford, *The protestant reformation in Ireland* (Frankfurt, 1985), pp 153-79.

74. P.R.O.N.I., T 520.

75. P.J.Corish, *The catholic community in the seventeenth and eighteenth centuries* (Dublin, 1981), p. 26.

76. This is based on Paul Walsh, *The will and family of Hugh O'Neill, earl of Tyrone* (Dublin, 1930).

77. For some implications of this situation see Gillespie, *Colonial Ulster*, pp 153-8.

78. *Cal. S.P. Ire., 1615-25*, p. 105; British Library, Additional Ms 39853, ff 2ᵛ, 6, 7ᵛ.

79. *Cal. S.P. Ire., 1615-25*, p. 71.

80. *Cal. S.P. Ire., 1615-25*, p. 407.

81. *Cal. S.P. Ire., 1615-25*, p. 69.

82. For a short biography of Davies, Hans Pawlisch, *Sir John Davies and the conquest of Ireland* (Cambridge,1985), pp 15-33.

83. F.E. Ball, *Judges in Ireland 1221-1921* (2 vols, London, 1926) i, pp 214, 252-4, 241; *Cal. S.P. Ire., 1608-10*, pp 420-4; *Cal. S.P. Ire., 1625-32*, p. 323.

84. Hill, *Plantation*, p. 589.

85. British Library, Additional Ms 4756, ff 118, 122ᵛ.

86. Chart, *Londonderry*, pp 131-2.

87. Gillespie, *Colonial Ulster*, pp 105, 210-11; there were frequent prosecutions in Castle Chamber for refusal to present recusants, H.M.C., *Egmont Mss*, 1, part i.

88. P.R.O.I., Ferguson Mss xi, p. 73. In general the practice in Ireland was similar to that in England described in J.S. Cockburn, *A history of the English assizes* (Cambridge, 1972), pp 65-133.

89. Gillespie, Colonial Ulster, pp 210-11.
90. Moody, *Londonderry plantation*, pp 282, 286-7.
91. Gillespie, *Colonial Ulster*, p. 103.
92. The jury is listed in the official record of the trial which was destroyed in 1922 but printed by Thomas Gogarty (ed.), 'Ulster roll of gaol delivery, 1615' in *Archivium Hibernicum* 6 (1917), pp 83-93.
93. Hill, *Plantation*, p. 322; Moody, *Londonderry plantation*, p. 448.
94. Moody, *Londonderry plantation*, pp 147, 170, 299.
95. Moody, *Londonderry plantation*, p. 157.
96. Moody, *Londonderry plantation*, pp 140, 280, 314-5, 317.
97. Moody and Simms (eds), *The bishopric of Derry* i, pp 91, 233, 317, 392-3, 414, 421; Moody, *Londonderry plantation*, pp 140, 280.
98. Moody, *Londonderry plantation*, p. 338; *Cal. S.P. Ire., 1608-10*, p. 367.
99. *Cal. S.P. Ire., 1615-25*, p. 375; Chart, *Londonderry*, p. 81.
100. Steele, *Tudor and Stuart proclamations*, 2, part i, no. 252. On native dress see D.B. Quinn, *The Elizabethans and the Irish* (Cornell, 1966), chapter 8.
101. This is based on a study of the Ulster port books in Leeds City Library, Temple Newsham Ms TN/PO7/I/1-4. The natives were often satirised for adopting these English habits, N.J.A. Williams (ed.), *Pairlement Chloinne Tomás* (Dublin, 1981).
102. Gogarty (ed.) 'Ulster roll of gaol delivery, 1615', pp 83-93.
103. P.R.O.I., RC12/1, RC6/1; P.R.O.N.I., T 475.
104. Tadhg Ó Donnchadha (ed.), *Leabhar Cloinne Aodha Buidhe* (Dublin, 1931), pp 166-71.
105. George Hill, *A historical account of the Macdonnells of Antrim* (Belfast, 1877), pp 284, 422; Maidment (ed), 'Letters and papers', p. 281.
106. *Inquisitionum in officio Rotulorum Cancellariae Hiberniae asservatarum repertorium* (Dublin, 1829) 2, Tyrone, James I no. 3; *Cal. pat. rolls Ire., Jas. I*, p. 355.
107. Brendan Jennings (ed.), *Wild Geese in Spanish Flanders, 1582-1700* (Dublin, 1964), pp 147, 148-9, 150, 151-2, 175.
108. Maidment (ed) 'Letters and papers', p. 281.
109. Moody, *Londonderry planatation*, p. 174.
110. *Cal. pat. rolls Ire., Jas. I*, p. 407; Moody, *Londonderry plantation*, p. 174.
111. Gilbert (ed.), *Contemporary history of affairs in Ireland*, i, p. 6.
112. Chart, *Londonderry*, p. 9.
113. Trumball's reports are printed in H.M.C., *Report on the Marquess of Downshire Mss* (4 vols, London, 1924-24), volume 2.
114. Canice Mooney, 'St. Anthony's College, Louvain' in *Donegal Annual* 8 (1969), pp 18-41; Grainne Henry, 'Seminarie soldiers: connections between religious and military communities in the Spanish Netherlands' in *Retrospect* 1987, pp 41-8.
115. Lambert McKenna (ed.), *Iomarbhágh na bFileadh* (2 vols, Irish texts society, London, 1918), i p. 126, 128.
116. John Hagan (ed.), 'Miscellanea Vaticano-Hibernica' in *Archivium Hibernicum* 4 (1915), p. 288.

117. Jesuit Archive, Leeson Street, Dublin, Annual Letters, 1615.

118. Jennings, *Wild geese*, pp 151-2; *Cal. S.P. Ire., 1615-25*, pp 97, 132, 133, 136.

119. David Rothe, *Analecta sacra...*, ed. P.F. Moran (Dublin, 1884), p. 38.

120. Philip O'Sullivan Beare, *Historiae Catholicae Hiberniae compendium*, ed. Matthew Kelly (Dublin, 1850), pp 334-5; for a short biography of O'Sullivan see T.J. O'Donnell (ed.), *Selections from the Zoilomastix of O'Sullivan Beare* (Dublin, 1960), pp iv-xv.

121. Geoffrey Keating, *Foras Feasa ar Éireann*, ed. David Comyn and P.S. Dineen (4 vols, Irish texts society, London, 1908-14), i pp 4-7.

122. Dominic O'Daly, *History of the Geraldines*, ed. C.P. Meehan (Dublin, 1847), pp 18-19.

123. National Library of Ireland, Ms 643; A.B. Grossart (ed.), *Lismore papers* (10 vols, London, 1886-8), 2nd series ii, p. 153.

124. Thomas Ryves, *Regininus Anglicania...* (Dublin, 1624); for a brief life of Ryves, B.P. Levack, *The civil lawyers in England 1603-41* (Oxford, 1973), p. 267.

125. *Cal. S.P. Ire., 1625-32*, pp 34-7.

126. British Library, Additional Ms 4770, f. 283. As Stephen Jerome, chaplain to the earl of Cork, commented Ireland 'wants nothing but religion, money and munitions', *Ireland's jubilee* (Dublin, 1624).

127. E.M. Jope, 'Moyry, Charlemont, Castleraw and Richhill: fortification to architecture in the north of Ireland, 1570-1700' in *Ulster Journal of Archaeology* 3rd ser. 23 (1960), pp 97-123.

128. Raymond Gillespie, 'The end of an era: Ulster and the outbreak on the 1641 rising' in Brady and Gillespie (eds), *Natives and newcomers*, pp 191-231.

129. Richard Bagwell, *Ireland under the Stuarts...* (3 vols, London 1909-16), i, p. 116.

130. E.A. d'Alton, *History of Ireland* (3 vols, Dublin 1912), ii, p. 224.

131. For Healy's background see Henry Boylan, *A dictionary of Irish biography* (Dublin, 1978), pp 141-2.

132. T.M. Healy, *The planters progress...to which is appended the victims of 1615* (Dublin, 1921), pp 42-71 deal with the conspiracy. MacInerney's letter is printed at the front of the volume.

133. Myles O'Reilly, *Memorials of those who suffered for the catholic faith in Ireland* (London, 1868), pp 183-4. There were also external sources to this movement since the bishops of Australasia wrote to their Irish counterparts in 1885 on the matter of the matyrdom of 'the saintly sons of Ireland', 'it will rejoice the hearts ...of the exiled children of St Patrick under the southern cross to see their heroic forefathers so gloriously honoured', Dublin Diocesan Archive, Beatifications etc, 1904-7, vol. 5, appendix.

134. The beatification procedure is summarised in W.J. Walsh, 'Canonisation of the Irish martyrs: the apostolic process' in *Irish Ecclesiastical Record* 5th ser. 9 (1918), pp 311-21; M.H. MacInerney, 'Archbishop Walsh and the Irish martyrs' in *Studies* 10 (1921), pp 178-90, 527-44.